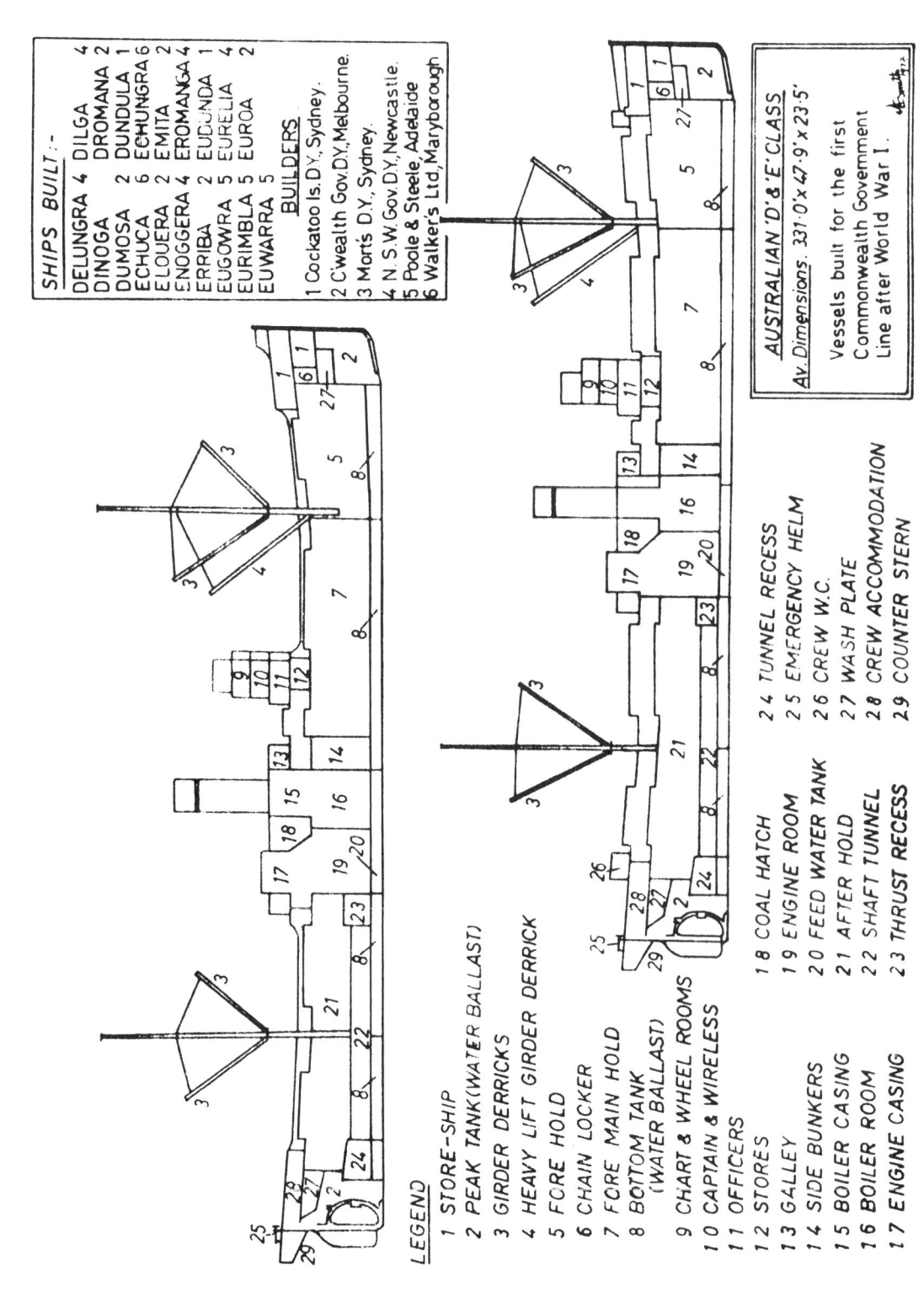

THE AUSTRALIAN COMMONWEALTH SHIPPING LINE

Roebuck Society Publication No. 20

First published 1978 at Canberra

National Library of Australia card number and
ISBN 0 909434 11 5

UNION OFFSET CO. PTY. LTD.
20 Pirie Street, Fyshwick, A.C.T. 2609

THE AUSTRALIAN COMMONWEALTH SHIPPING LINE

by

FRANK BRENNAN

A ROEBUCK BOOK

ROEBUCK SERIES

This title comes from the name of HMS *Roebuck*, the ship in which Captain William Dampier, the first Englishman to describe part of Australia, made his second visit to Australia. On this voyage he sighted the Western Australian coast at Shark Bay, on 6 August 1699, and followed it to the northeast to Roebuck Bay. Having failed to find water he then left the coast for Timor, afterwards visiting the north coast of New Guinea.

This series is intended to provide an outlet for books of merit on Australian historical subjects

Issued in this series

1. Kangaroo Island, 1800-1836. By J.S. Cumpston, D. Litt.
2. Captain Cook's Australian Landfalls. By W.D. Forsyth, M.A. (Melb.) B.Litt. (Oxon.)
3. King Island and the Sealing Trade, 1802. By Helen Mary Micco, B.A.
4. Watch off Arnhem Land. By C.T.G. Haultain.
5. The Furneaux Group. First Visitors, 1797-1810. By J.S. Cumpston, D. Litt.
6. Kangaroo Island Shipwrecks. By G.D. Chapman.
7. First Visitors to Bass Strait. By J.S. Cumpston, D. Litt.
8. To Botany Bay. By R.A. Swan, B.A.
9. Augustus Gregory and the Inland Sea. By J.H.L. Cumpston, M.D.
10. Gundaroo. By E.J. Lea-Scarlett, B.A.
11. The Sydney Gazette, Volume 9, 1811. Facsimile.
12. The Long Arm. By Hugh V. Clarke.
13. Wheels in the Storm. By W. Aron, M.B.E., B.A. (Cantab).
14. Memories of Hall. By Leon R. Smith.
15. Captain Eber Bunker. By R. Hodgkinson, M.B.M.S.
16. Bunbury. By Theodora Sanders.
19. The Health of the People. By J.H.L. Cumpston, C.M.G., M.D.
22. Shipping Arrivals and Departures, Sydney, Vol. 1, 1788-1825. by J.S. Cumpston.
23. Shipping Arrivals and Departures, Sydney, Vol. 2, 1826-1840. By Captain I.H. Nicholson, R.A.N.

This is No. 20 in the series, all of which are obtainable from booksellers, or from J.S. Cumpston 42 Araba Street, Aranda, A.C.T. 2614.

THE AUSTRALIAN COMMONWEALTH SHIPPING LINE

CONTENTS

Chapter		Page
1.	Introduction	1
2.	General History of the Australian Commonwealth Shipping Line	2
3.	The Austral Ships	18
4.	The German Ships	27
5.	Coal Burning Ships	35
6.	Sailing Ships and Vessels	39
7.	The American Purchase. Wooden Motor Vessels and Steamers	41
8.	The "D" and "E" Class Ships	42
9.	The Bay Ships	48
10.	Australia's Largest Coastal Ship	51
11.	The "Dale" Ships	53
12.	Migration	54
13.	Epilogue	56
	Appendix A — The Commonwealth Fleet on 31 July 1923	61
	Appendix B — Mr Bruce's First Financial Statement, showing position of Commonwealth Fleet as at 30 June, 1923	63
	Appendix C — Mr Bruce's Second Financial Statement, showing position of Commonwealth Fleet as at 31 March 1928	64

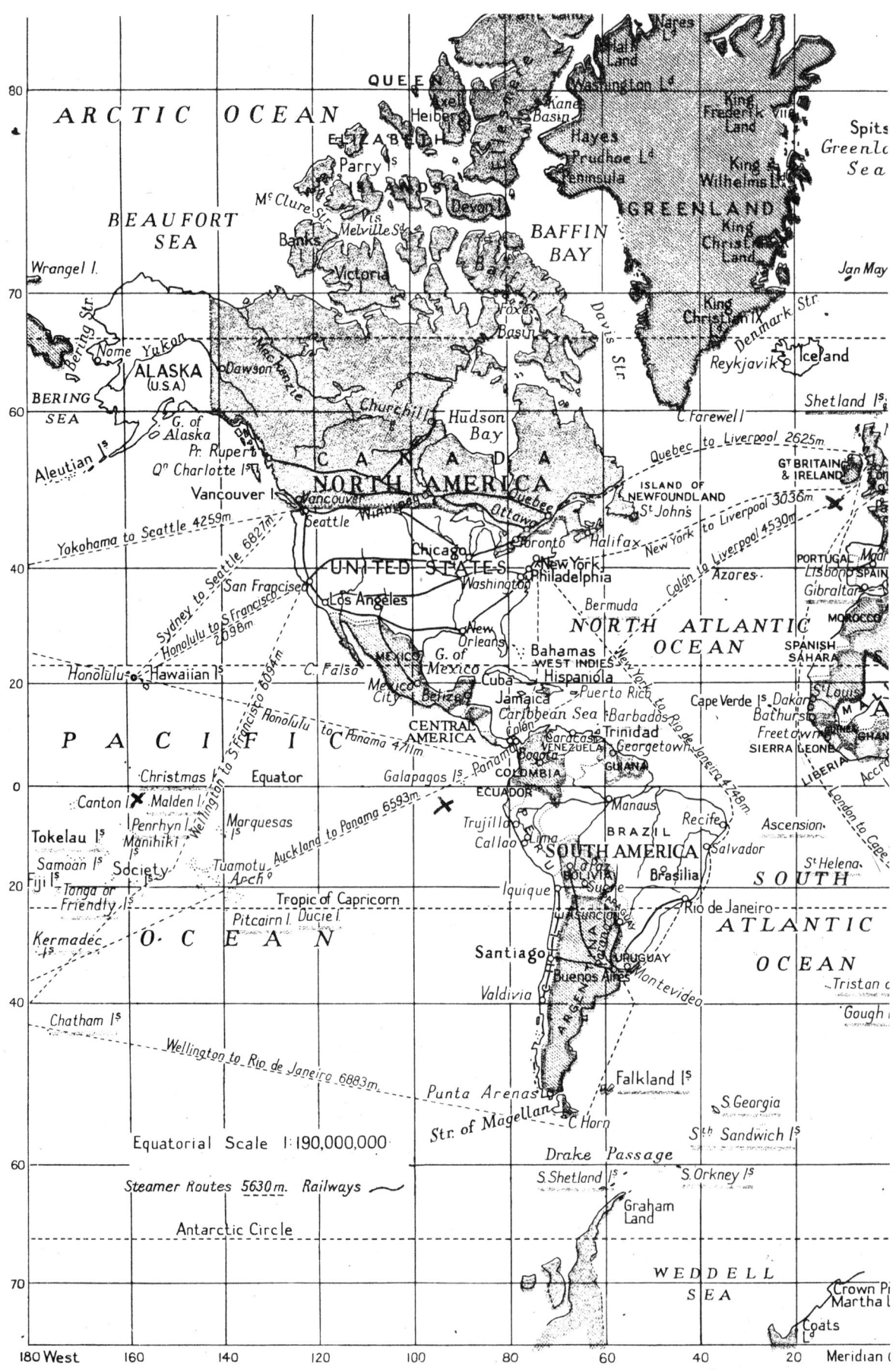

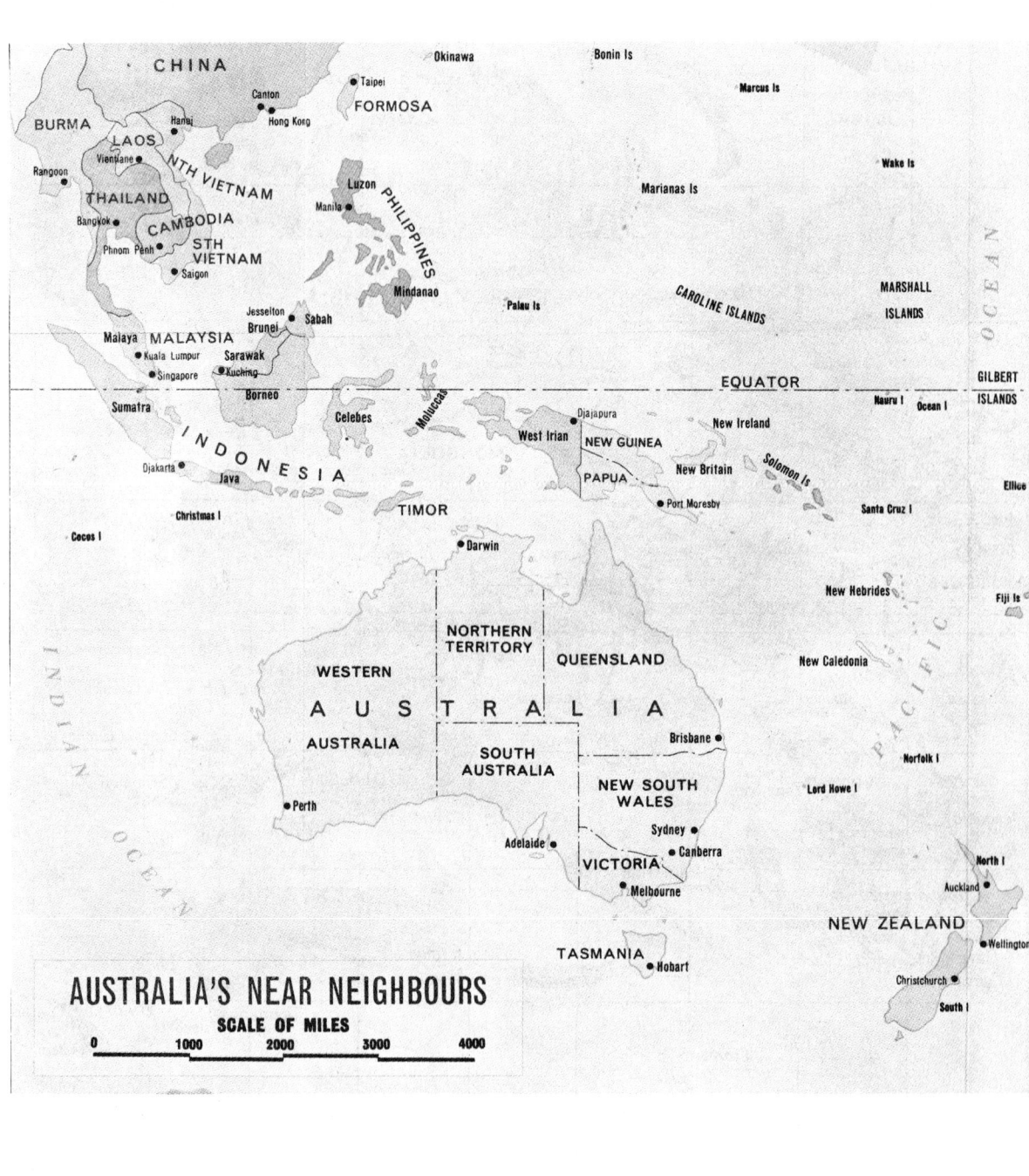

Chapter 1

INTRODUCTION

Having written the story of the Commonwealth Line in a condensed form, I can hardly regard it as a history. To have told the story in full would require several volumes: the details of the shipbrokers' transactions in the purchase of the "Strath" ships, the American contracts for the building of the wooden ships, the various systems of requisitioning of the German ships; all representing much documentation and most of it unavailable to the researcher. Even with the Australian built "E" class and "D" class ships, information is hard to come by. Walkers Ltd. of Maryborough, Queensland, lost many of their records in a fire some years ago. With the aid of Lloyds Shipping Registers and many volumes of old newspapers, I believe I have secured an accurate account of the snips of the Commonwealth Fleet.

During the years of the First World War, ships sailed under sealed orders; their departures and arrivals were never publicised. I heard much about the ships of the Commonwealth Line, and those who went down to the sea in them, from seafarers in various forecastles during my early days at sea. Much of this information was suspect — sailors always talked of their last ship as being the best ever, and the one they happened to be on at the time as the worst possible — a compensating balance of nature I suppose. The miseries of a Western Ocean winter crossing housed in the bows of a pitching tramp steamer are banished into the past once the Liverpool Pier Head is abeam. Though conditions on the Australian ships were far superior to those of any other country, the Commonwealth Line seemed to have more than their share of crew troubles. In those faded newspapers of 50 years ago, the incidence of delayed sailings through this cause is repeated with monotonous regularity. However, as I intend the story to be accurate and incidents factual, I shall refrain from repeating "dogwatch" gossip.

To complete the result of my months of research, I have compiled in some detail the histories of the various ships. To relate these, I must, of necessity, repeat some of the facts about the ships mentioned briefly in the general history of the Line. It was my interest in ships and the sea that prompted this research and so I must cater for the student of maritime history, yet keep the technicalities to a minimum. As crew troubles played such a large part in the failure of the Commonwealth Line, my own opinion, after hearing so many accounts of the unbridgeable gap between labour and management, is given for what it is worth.

At the time of the Line's expansion with the building of the "D" class and "E" class cargo ships, Navy demobilisation was taking place. Quite a large number of ex-navy officers were given appointments in the Commonwealth Line ships. In the Navy brevity is the keynote of all orders, and with the full weight of the Naval

Discipline Act and K.R. & A.I. (Kings Rules and Admiralty Instructions) behind them, the giving of orders by officers and acquiescence thereto by the ratings presented no problems. In the merchant ships the ex-Navy officers found themselves at a great disadvantage. The maximum penalty that could be imposed on any recalcitrant member of the crew was a "logging" and a fine of five shillings. This could only be done by the ship's master and inevitably led to more trouble. Australian ships were not allowed to sail without a full crew, so the absence of one man was enough to keep a ship tied up to the wharf. Replacements could only be supplied by the Seamen's Union, who expressed "difficulty" in doing so, should the ship, its captain or officers not be approved by the Union. Some ex-Navy officers accepted the position as it was, others did not, arguing that what worked under the white ensign should work under the red ensign. Other Australian based shipping companies did not have the same difficulties, as their officers having served their time as apprentices or cadets, had worked alongside seamen, doing the same tasks. Consequently, when reaching officer rank, they knew the ships, the working thereof, and above all, the crew's reactions to various situations. In addition to this, Australian coastal shipping companies had built up certain traditions over the years, inspiring a degree of loyalty among the crews which seemed to be lacking in the Commonwealth Line.

Chapter 2

GENERAL HISTORY OF THE AUSTRALIAN COMMONWEALTH SHIPPING LINE.

Lloyds Shipping Register 1916-17 shows that the Commonwealth Government had only one ship registered under their ownership. This was the twin screw steamer *Merimbula*, registered at the Port of Sydney, a supply ship controlled by the Administrator of the Northern Territory. She was a handy vessel, fitted to carry some refrigerated cargo, and her dimensions and origin were as follows:- gross tonnage 1,111 tons, net tonnage 455 tons, length 209' 6", breadth 32'2", depth 21'1".

Builders were the Ailsa Ship Building Company of Troon. She left the Clyde on her delivery voyage in June 1909. *Merimbula* could be acknowledged as the pioneer of the Commwealth Government Line of steamers, the address of the head office being Australia House, London. The meteoric rise and fall of this short lived shipping line, whose fleet at one period consisted of 62 ocean going ships, is now almost forgotten history. It first appeared on Lloyds Register of 1917-18, and by 1929 ceased to exist.

The only vessels registered under Commonwealth Government ownership for 1929 were two naval colliers *Biloela* and *Kurumba*, one Trade and Customs vessel *Lady Loch*, and five lighthouse tenders, *Cape Leeuwin, Cape York, Lienta, Karuah,* and *Kyogle*. The ships which had comprised the fleet were sold and found employment in various parts of the world. When visiting Australian ports the waterside fraternity always recognised and referred to them as "Billy Hughes' ships". To give the full story of the Commonwealth Line, some space must be given to its founder, William Morris Hughes. Numerous books have been compiled on the life of this controversial statesman who, though born in London, became known as one of the "Great" Australians, a legend in his own lifetime. During his colourful and varied career, ships and those who manned them held some fascination for him. In these pages I can only give passing mention to his career on the maritime scene.

William Morris Hughes was born in Pimlico, London on 25th September, 1864, both parents coming from Wales. They returned to Llandudno in 1870. After a few years the family came back to London. Hughes completed his education at a school in Westminster, afterwards securing a post as pupil teacher there at a salary of ten pounds per annum. His main hobbies were rowing and bellringing. Later he joined the Militia, serving in the Royal Fusiliers. An opportunity occurred to work with the Dogger Bank Fishing Fleet. This decided him to seek broader horizons than the walls of a London school room. He applied for an assisted passage to Australia and boarded the Ducal Line ship *Duke of Westminster*. The Ducal Line in conjunction with the British India Steamship Co., and the Queensland Government, maintained a regular steamship service connecting London with all Queensland ports via Torres Straits. *Duke of Westminster* (Captain Long) was a vessel of 2,147 tons net. A total of 457 passengers, and a large and varied cargo were delivered to Thursday Island, Cooktown, Townsville, Keppel Bay, and Hervey Bay, and the ship finally arrived in Moreton Bay on 8 December 1884. Hughes and his fellow passengers completed their journey to Brisbane on the paddle tug *Boko*.

Hughes was not impressed with Brisbane, or the Immigration Depot which he likened to a decrepit London workhouse. There were many unemployed in Brisbane and, within a few days, Hughes rolled his swag and commenced some years of wandering around Queensland. During this time he accumulated enough sea time to get an A.B.'s discharge and served as fireman on river steamers. The Gympie gold fields attracted him ashore. In all gold rushes there are more losers than winners, and Hughes failed to get enough gold to provide the bare essentials. He found his way to the coast at Noosa, and took passage to Brisbane on the paddle steamer *Adonis* where he enlisted as a private in the Queensland militia. The "Russian Scare" of that period kept him fully employed; part of his service being at Thursday Island with instructions to blow up the coal hulks anchored there should a Russian warship appear on the scene. Hughes then signed on as a cook on the A.S.N. Co. *Maranoa*. This vessel was then on the Melbourne to Burketown passenger and cargo run. His cooking ability failed to give satisfaction, and Hughes was demoted to pantryman. On the ship's return to Sydney he asked for and was granted a discharge. Australia was then on the verge of bankruptcy, employment was scarce and wages poor. Hughes settled in Pyrmont and soon became a familiar figure along "The Hungry Mile" of the **Sussex Street wharves**. His leadership was recognised by the Maritime Unions, and the Great Strike of 1890 gave Hughes a reputation as a tough negotiator. In the settlement of this dispute he earned the respect of all concerned, and the road opened for a political career.

April 1907 saw Hughes at sea once again on his way to represent Australia at the Imperial Conference in London. This time he travelled first class on the R.M.S. *Orient*. Returning via America, he crossed the Atlantic on R.M.S. *Baltic* and joined s.s. *Aorangi* at San Francisco for the voyage to Sydney. The luxury travel was a contrast to the dormitory accommodation in the tween decks of the

Duke of Westminster, or the "Foc'sles" and "Glory Holes" of the Australian coasters. In August 1914, Andrew Fisher, Australia's Prime Minister, with the full support of his cabinet, pledged Australia to the last man, and the last shilling There was nothing half hearted about Australia's war effort. In a matter of three days ships were converted into troop carriers. Most of the country's large coastal passenger ships were refitted as troopers and hospital ships. Cargo ships were taken over as colliers to serve with the Australian Navy. The first shot of World War 1 was fired in Australia. Some hours before war was declared, the German steamer *Pfalz* had left the Melbourne wharves to get clear before the hostilities started. The battery at Queenscliff put a shot across her bows which was ignored. Meanwhile, on the bridge of the *Pfalz,* the Port Philip Pilot had started a war of his own, and when his advice to the Captain had no effect and *Pfalz* continued to steam towards the heads, he took direct action and, after a brief tussle, convinced the ship's master of his error of judgment.

Pfalz was a fine new ship of 6,750 tons gross, launched in 1913. Eleven other German ships were interned in Australian ports, and these were taken over by the British Director of Shipping who placed them under the management of the Commonwealth Government. These ships, by virtue of their colour scheme, were known as "The Black Germans" and took stores, horses and fodder in the wake of the first troop convoy which left Australia in October 1914. The German ships served at the Dardanelles landing, and were later used to evacuate the sick and wounded from Gallipoli to hospitals in Egypt. Aboard one of these, s.s. *Hessen* was Norman Gilroy, who had signed on in Melbourne as wireless operator. After completing time at sea, he joined the priesthood and reached the eminence of Cardinal in the Australian Catholic Church. As the fleet list shows, the oldest of the German ships was only 15 years old, a handy size for world trading, They later joined the fleet of the Australian Commonwealth Line. Meanwhile, back in Australia, wool and wheat were accumulating. An assured market existed in Europe and there were no ships to get it there. On 27 October 1915 Andrew Fisher resigned as Prime Minister, and William Morris Hughes took over as head of Government. Andrew Fisher went to London as Australian High Commissioner.

Though the British Government had bought and paid for the Australian wool and wheat crop, and had assumed control of shipping, they did not have the power to direct ship-owners, who had formed a combine, to divert ships to uneconomic routes. Vessels previously engaged on the Australian cargo routes, which had a capacity of 252,000 tons, had been withdrawn. These ships were now placed on the shorter and more profitable trans-Atlantic routes. As the whole of Britain's factory production was geared to war requirements, cargoes available to Australian bound ships would be hard to find, and one way ballast voyages for such a long haul would not produce a healthy balance sheet. With a full year's wheat crop in temporary storage, and another crop ready to harvest, Hughes decided to go to England and break the deadlock. On this occasion he travelled via Canada and America, and embarked on the Red star liner *Finland* in New York, arriving at Liverpool on 7 March 1916. At this period of the war Britain was passing through some of its darkest hours, and there was no sign of the dawn. Huge losses in shipping, the full realisation of the U Boat peril, starvation rations, the Dardanelles evacuation, the stalemate of trench warfare with heavy casualties, these and many other factors had left Britain's morale somewhat battered. Asquith, always urbane, always the gentleman, with his oft repeated assurance to "wait and see", could be compared with Neville Chamberlain who found himself in a somewhat similar position 24 years later. The British people were disenchanted, and looked for a dynamic leader who would guide them out of the morass.

The arrival of William Morris Hughes in Britain, with his fervour and patriotism, and his unpolished eloquence, was taken up by the press. Invitations poured in from every part of the country to speak at assemblies of all kinds. He was hailed as the great hope of the British Empire. His main mission was ships; within hours of his arrival he saw Asquith, whom he summed up in the few words "Too much Cicero and too little Caesar". Asquith was courteous but regretful that nothing could be done and arranged for Hughes to see Mr Runciman. The results of this interview were negative, but the Australian Prime Minister was allowed to plead his case before Sir Joseph Maclay, Director of Shipping, who, in turn, referred him to a committee of shipping experts. This committee was comprised entirely of ship owners, and Hughes' eloquence had no effect on this august body. Their summing up was a brief "impossible". Hughes reply to this was "Nothing is impossible in time of war, and as you won't help me I'll help myself". On leaving the meeting, Hughes clinched the deal which he had started a few days previously. With the connivance of Andrew Fisher, by then well established as High Commissioner at Australia House, Hughes met a shipbroker and arranged the purchase of 25 ships, the name of the purchaser to remain a closely guarded secret. Though all these ships were on charter to the British Government at the time, advantage was taken of a cancellation clause which existed should change of ownership take place. The news of this acquisition came as a bombshell to the Governments of both Britain and Australia.

The owners of ten of these ships, whose sale conditions had not been finalised, immediately cancelled the sale. They had been under the impression the ships were being purchased for a member of the shipping combine. However for the other 15 ships the deal had gone through. Runciman threatened to confiscate the ships as soon as they arrived at British Ports, but in this matter he could not get Asquith's support. At the next meeting of the two Prime Ministers, Asquith told Hughes he could keep his ships, after getting an assurance that there would be no more similar transactions. The British public, always admirers of "Men of Action" gave the shipping deal their full support. During his short stay in Britain Hughes received the freedom of 7 major cities. Petitions were signed by many thousands asking him to stay in Britain and take his place in the War Cabinet. Further inducements came from official sources. Hughes went over to France and spent some time with the Australian troops in their front line positions. He was tireless in his campaign to find out the true position on the Western front. He had many virtues, but patience was not one of them. Wherever he travelled he ignored 'red tape' and officialdom. He sought the opinions of Privates as well as Generals and for the remainder of his life was known as "The Little Digger".

His shipping mission accomplished, and the Commonwealth Line duly registered at Australia House under the management of Mr H.G.B. Larkin, Hughes sailed for Australia. The shipping deal, whilst hailed by many as a stroke of genius, also had its critics, chiefly amongst the Opposition members of the Federal Parliament.

Mr Cook, the Opposition Leader, pointed out that there were two million tons of wheat on hand. The 15 ships would only be able to move 300,000 tons of this in one year. Other points of his criticism were that the ships were not suitable for such voyages, and most of them had been worked with Asiatic crews and the existing accommodation would not comply with the Australian Commonwealth Navigation Act. He summarised as follows — "The buying of the ships may be carrying out Labor's policy but it is not carrying away our wheat. He could only look with suspicion on the deal, as something to help expropriation of capital, which is Labor's policy". In the light of subsequent events, such criticism was unjustified. In spite of modest freight charges, the ships paid for themselves within two years.

An examination of the deal in closer detail is warranted. The 15 ships as per listing were renamed and registered at the various Australian Ports; each of the names was preceded by "AUSTRAL" and they became known as the Austral ships. Ten of the ships were purchased from one Company — Messrs. Burrell & Sons of Glasgow. They were the "Strath" ships, quite modern and good cargo carriers, of similar tonnage and dimensions. The other 5 ships came from various owners — the oldest being *Dalton Hall*, launched in 1899; in brief, they were good solid unspectacular ships, such as one could see by the score under the coal tips of Swansea or Cardiff, or the wheat silos of Montreal. The average tonnage of the 15 ships was 4,145 gross and 2,725 net. Their pre-War price was £4 per ton (dead weight): Australia paid £19 per ton, a total of £2,068,000, the larger ships being £140,000 each. By World standards at the time, the price was quite a reasonable one. Shipping losses due to enemy action were catastrophic. The sinkings reached the figure of 50 a week. The introduction of the convoy system under David Lloyd George's Prime Ministership later reduced the loss figures dramatically.

On board ship on his way home to Australia, Hughes was not idle. He realised that Australia must not be placed in such a weak position again and that the only answer was a Commonwealth ship building programme. Perhaps he recalled the words of Themistocles, the Athenian Statesman, Orator and Commander of 2,400 years ago: "He who commands the sea has command of everything". The Lloyds Register 1916-17 included the 12 German ships interned at the outbreak of the War as requisitioned by the Australian Government and registered at London. The names had been changed to those with aboriginal content, starting with the letters B or C, the one exception being *Parattah* ex *Berlin*. These ships joined the "Australs" in the huge task of freighting Australia's produce to Europe. Some criticism was made of the circuitous routes taken but with a world wide shortage of tonnage, cargoes were easy to obtain, and a diversion of a few hundred miles carrying paying cargo instead of rubble ballast was good business. Other additions to the Commonwealth Government fleet were the hopper dredge *Sir William Mathews* of 1389 tons gross, built 1914 by Fleming and Ferguson of Paisley and the coal hulk *Shandon. Shandon*, formerly a four masted barque built in 1883, was a staunch iron built vessel, which after many years of trading around the world, was relegated to an anchorage in the quiet waters of Sydney Harbour. *Shandon* also saw service in World War II. She was towed from Adelaide to Townsville to act as bunkering station for troopships.

On his return to Australia, Hughes arranged with the existing shipyards in Australia to build standardised cargo vessels. These facilities were at Newcastle, N.S.W., Williamstown in Victoria, and Cockatoo Dock in Sydney. Orders were placed for 6 of these ships to be known as "D" Class. As these vessels and their later counterparts were to play a large part in Australia's maritime development, a brief description of them is warranted:- single screw, steel built, shelter deck type, length between perpendiculars 331 feet, breadth 47 feet 9 inches and depth 23 feet 6 inches and a carrying capacity of 6,000 tons. The ships had a gross tonnage of 3346 tons and net tonnage of 1934 tons. The cast iron propeller 16 feet in diameter, was designed to give the vessel a service speed of 10 knots. They were built to the highest of Lloyd's specifications with the Isherwood system of longitudinal framing. A straight stem and an elliptical stern with a flush deck gave a rather pleasing hull shape.

The hull had a flat keel plate and a double bottom forming six tanks with a watertight fore and aft bulkhead. Though the ships were designed as coal burners, provision was made for some of the tanks to hold oil fuel, should conversion be made at a later date. There were 4 main cargo hatches and a cross bunker hatch abaft the bridge superstructure, with a coaling hatch on each side for the pocket bunkers. Refrigeration space of 11,000 cubic feet was provided but as access to this was through the bunker hatch, care had to be taken to avoid cargo contamination from coal dust. The engines were triple expansion, the cylinders being 25 inches, 41 inches and 68 inches with a stroke of 45 inches. Developing 2,000 indicated horse power these engines were quite massive, weighing over 100 tons, measuring 21 feet in length and 16 feet in width, the height from foot plate to cylinder tops being 23 feet. Steam was generated in 3 tubulous boilers, with a working pressure of 180 lbs. per square inch. A new innovation was the Mitchell Thrust Block with its single collar on which the whole thrust of the propellor is taken. For cargo handling, 11 winches were fitted to operate 12 derricks, one over No. 2 hold being designed for heavy lifts up to 20 tons. Two lifeboats and a cutter were carried for the crew of 37. These ships were designed for Australia's extensive coastal trade though capable of overseas voyages. Their design was austere but built to work and last under rugged conditions. Some of them completed over 30 years service under various owners before going to the shipbreakers.

The building of the 6 'D' class ships was a long process; skilled labour had to be trained and machines built and installed. The cost worked out to be just double that of similar ships being built in the U.K. shipyards. *Delungra* was delivered by the Newcastle builders in 1919, followed by *Dilga* and *Dinoga* in 1920. These 3 vessels were registered at their birth place. Williamstown Dockyards delivered *Dromana* in 1919, *Dumosa* in 1920, and Sydney completed *Dundula* in 1920. Orders were placed for a further 13 of these ships. In addition to the established yards which had built the 6 D Class, Messrs Walkers Ltd. of Maryborough, Queensland, and Messrs. Poole & Steel of Adelaide took part in the building program.

Realising that Australian ship building could not develop in time to deal with immediate shipping requirements, Hughes turned to America where standardised ships were being built on the assembly line principle. These were a product of the American Pacific Coast Ports, mainly Patterson and Macdonald and the Sloan shipyard of Seattle. Some of these vessels were motor ships, others steamships, all wooden built, twin screw, engines aft, 2,368 gross tonnage and 1,820 net tonnage. Other dimensions were length 262 feet 2 inches, breadth 46 feet 4 inches, and depth 21 feet. In the case of steamships they were fitted with two water tube boilers. The Australian Government ordered 11 of these ships, which were duly delivered in 1918. Once again the nomenclature was distinctly Australian and commenced with the letters B & C: *Culburra, Challamba, Cethana,*

Babinda, Bellata, Benowa, Berriga, Bethanga, Birriwa, Bundarra and *Coolcha*. These ships were registered at the various Australian Ports. The P. & O. Branch line, successors to Wm. Lund's Blue Anchor Line, also gave Australian names to their ships. Each commenced with the letter 'B', some little difference to the names given to the new additions to the Government Fleet, adding to the task of the researcher.

Surprisingly little is known of the 11 wooden ships; they appear in Lloyd's list of 1920 but none were there in the 1924-25 list. They scarcely received a mention in the shipping lists of the newspapers of the period, and appeared to spend more time in dockyard hands than at sea. Built as a war time expedient, their timbers unseasoned and design untested, the hulls of these ships leaked and shippers would not trust their cargoes in them. Old time seamen recalled them as ships to be avoided. I believe some were sold as Pacific Island Traders, but their wooden construction, mainly oregon pine, made them susceptible to the depredations of borers and other destructive pests. The last two of these ships were burnt in Sydney Harbour in 1928, after years of idleness.

A segment and certainly the main feature of the Australian Government shipping line was providing for the post war migration programme. In 1918 plans were drawn up for the building of 5 passenger cargo liners. The design of these ships fulfilled all immediate and foreseeable future requirements, and they were destined to play a large part in Australia's development and are worthy of a chapter in this history of the Commonwealth Line.

As the War drew to a close, further German ships were handed over to the Commonwealth Government. By 1920 the German section of the fleet had increased to 20. This included one sailing vessel *Cardinia,* ex *Olinda*. One of the few sailing ships listed 100 A 1 in Lloyd's Register, she had been built in 1903, of steel construction, 1915 tons, length 264 feet, breadth 40 feet, depth 29 feet 9 inches. Whilst under Australian management, *Cardinia* was registered in Sydney. The builders were A. Rodger & Co., Glasgow. How she came to be under the German Flag is a mystery. The Commonwealth Line only had this vessel for just over a year. Research regarding her ultimate fate has yielded no result. Two other interesting additions to the fleet during 1920 were two 5 masted barquentines. These sister ships were built of wood by Messrs Kidman and Mayoh on the Parramatta River. They were launched in 1919; 1800 tons gross, length 250 feet, breadth 45 feet, depth 21 feet. They were given the names *Braeside* and *Burnside*. These locally built ships made little contribution to Australia's economy and disappeared from the local scene after a year's service. The immediate post war years brought an end to lucrative freight rates, revealing a huge surplus of tramp ships. Hughes had resigned as Prime Minister on January 5th, 1918. The issue which brought this about was total conscription and so has nothing to do with this history. However, the foundation stone of the Australian Commonwealth Shipping Line had been well and truly laid and plans completed for full expansion.

A post war debate on the future of the line was held in the Federal Parliament on 25th June 1919. Patriotism carried the day and it was decided to complete the expansion as planned. In 1920 the "E" class cargo ships joined the "D" class prototypes. The Naval Dockyard in Sydney delivered *Eudunda*. Newcastle completed *Eurelia* a few months later. Walkers of Queensland finalised work on *Echuca* and had *Echunga* ready for launching. Messrs Poole & Steele of Adelaide handed over *Eurimbla* and laid the keel of *Euwarra*. *Elouera* in Sydney

1. *Loch Ryan* in dry dock.

2. *Shandon*

EX-GERMAN SHIPS

3. s.s. *Tarawa* ex *Tural* Wrecked 21 March 1920.

4. s.s. *Boonah* ex s.s. *Melbourne*.

5. s.s. *Barambah* ex s.s. *Hobart*.

6. s.s. *Booral* ex s.s. *Oberhausen*. In war time camouflage paint.

7. Port Phillip Pilot Ship *Akuna*. Formerly s.s. *Una*, Australian Commonwealth Line. Previously German s.s. *Komet*.

AUSTRAL SHIPS

8. s.s. *Australcrag* ex *Strathleven*. Showing camouflage paint.

was the last of this class to be delivered early in 1924, making a total of 20 of these ships. Further orders had been placed, including two with Walkers Ltd. The orders for these ships were cancelled: the post war shipping boom had been of short duration. Established shipping lines were fighting hard to build up services on a pre-war schedule. The Tramp companies suffered the most and in the various estuaries around Britain ships were moored with one watchman for several vessels. *Gareloch*, in the Clyde approaches *Blackwater* in Essex and the *Thames* off Southend Pier, these unwanted craft were to spend years awaiting employment, their only use being a roosting place for the seagulls.

In Australia, the position was somewhat worse. The Australian seaman had a 48 hour week; his English counterpart worked 84 hours per week before overtime was applicable. A clause in the Board of Trade Agreement gave the shipowners further benefits. No overtime was payable on the day of sailing and the day of arrival at any port; thus on a tramping voyage there were many such days. A qualified A.B. or Fireman was paid £9 per month, without annual leave or statutory holidays. Lascar crews received less than half this amount. Australian crews were paid £18 per month, plus other benefits which sounded like paradise to seafarers in other parts of the world. Under these circumstances the ships of the Commonwealth Fleet could not compete on the world trade routes. The first of the "Australs" to go was *Australstream*, ex *Dalton Hall*, the oldest of the ships built by Furness Withy & Co. West Hartlepool, in 1899. She left Australia bearing the name *General Degoute*. The same year (1921) *Australfield* ex *Vermont*, a product of Barclay Currie & Co. of Glasgow in 1900, sailed away to continue her hardworking life as *Liberta*. The most modern ship of the Hughes London purchase, *Australport* ex *Ardongorm*, built in 1915 by Napier and Miller of Glasgow, was transferred to the then expanding fleet of Broken Hill Pty. Ltd. early in 1925. Only *Australbrook*, *Australmead* and *Australplain* remained in the fleet. A year later *Australplain* was the sole survivor. Early in 1926 she also left for Eastern waters. Japan was then embarking on a policy of empire expansion and most of the *Australs* were purchased by Japanese shipping companies. As the fate of the Commonwealth Line depended on world shipping freight charges, a few figures make the picture clearer.

Early in 1914 the freight charge for coal from Cardiff to Port Said was 6s. 4½d. per ton. By 1915 this had risen to 68s. 9d. per ton and later to £10 per ton. During this period, seamen's wages rose to £11 per month, firemen to £12 per month. By the end of 1921, the freight rate for coal ex Cardiff to Port Said was 11s.3d. per ton. Seafarers' wages dropped by £2.10s.0d. per month. Voyage profit figures also show how short the boom period was. The figures represent profit in percentages of the Pound Sterling, related to 1 ton, in deadweight measurement.

In 1910:- 0.5% with a steady increase to 2.6% in 1913, followed by a decline in 1914 to 1.9%. A sharp rise took place in 1916 when 5.5% was reached. This continued to 1920 when the peak of 5.7% was attained. The collapse came very quickly. By 1925, the profit was down to 1.1% reaching a low of 0.3% in 1930 by which time 3½ million tons of British shipping was laid up.

In 1920 orders had been placed by the Commonwealth Line for two large all purpose cargo ships to be called *Ferndale* and *Fordsdale*. The order was placed with the Cockatoo Island Shipyard in Sydney. They were designed as a challenge to the post war building of the lines which for many years had maintained regular cargo services between Australia and U.K., the Scottish Shire Line, New Zealand

Shipping Co., Federal Steam Navigation Co., Clan Line, and the Commonwealth and Dominion Line, better known as the Port Line. The building of the two sister ships, *Ferndale* and *Fordsdale*, was slow and costly. They were the largest ships built in Australia, a record surpassed only a few years ago with the building of bulk carriers. *Ferndale* and *Fordsdale* both registered in Melbourne, were ships of 9,674 tons gross and 5.661 tons net. They were designed to trade to all ports serviced by the established companies. This included the Port of Manchester 35½ miles from the Mersey Port of Eastham. Five sets of locks had to be negotiated, 600 feet in length and 65 feet in width. The width of "The Dales" was restricted to 62 feet. After many trials and tribulations *Fordsdale* sailed on her maiden voyage early in 1924, and managed to reach the Port of Manchester. Her passage through the canal and the locks caused such concern to the canal pilot and the masters of the two assisting tugs that the experiment was never repeated. The ships had large refrigerated holds and loading gear to handle all types of cargo. The length of time building, whilst freight rates decreased, was a financial disaster for the Commonwealth Line. They serviced all the main Australian Ports and their regular voyages to the United Kingdom were made via the Suez. The 5 "Bay" ships ordered at the same time from British builders were delivered on schedule. *Moreton Bay*, registered at Brisbane, and built by Vickers of Barrow, arrived in Brisbane on January 19th, 1922. *Largs Bay* arrived a month later. The last to be delivered was *Esperance Bay*. The ships were well planned and well built and their subsequent performance amply justified the hopes of the Committee of Federal Parliamentarians who gave the word to go ahead with their construction. At this juncture we shall leave the "Dales" and "Bays" and return to the pioneer ships of the line.

The interned German ships had only been placed under the management of the Commonwealth Line. Later, when joined by other German Reparations Ships, the management was altered to a sort of lend lease agreement. Some of these ships were top class cargo liners and had sailed under the flag of the Deutsche Australische Company. In the original plan of the Commonwealth Line regular services were to be provided for Australasia including the Pacific Islands. *Boorara* ex *Pfalz*, built in 1913, was used to help establish this. Some of the smaller American-built wooden ships were also used on this service. They were *Bellata, Berringa, Bethanga, Birriwa,* and *Bundarra*. It was a losing battle: high wages, expensive repairs and other factors defeated branching out into the Pacific, whose broad expanses were left to the ships of Burns Philip & Co. Their ships were registered in London and their crews recruited in Singapore. The second part of the plan was the European service. This was to be taken care of with some success by the "Bays" and "Dales". During 1925 10% of Australia's produce was exported in ships of the Commonwealth Line. The third phase was the establishment of a 3 weekly service from Sydney to Singapore via Java. *Bambra* ex *Prinz Zigmund* and *Bakara* ex *Cannstatt* saw some service on this run. It is noted that only German ships with refrigeration spaces were chosen to take part in the bid for Eastern trade. Like the Australasia project, this also proved a failure, and the ships of Ellerman Bucknall took over. Like most sections of the Ellerman Group, Lascars were employed on deck, stokehold and engine room duties. In spite of this financial advantage, they also failed to make a success of the Java-Singapore venture. Having made this somewhat sketchy history of the early years of the Commonwealth Line, I will return to the Line's founder, William Morris Hughes, whose political career ran parallel with the ebb and flow of the Shipping Line's fortunes.

As I have already mentioned, Hughes tendered his resignation to the Governor General on January 6th, 1918. The usual procedure is for the outgoing Prime Minister to advise the Governor General regarding his successor, but Hughes was an unusual man and kept silent on the subject. Sir John Forrest was asked to form a Government, but a rapid assessment revealed he would not have enough support. In this unique situation the onus of overcoming the deadlock was placed in the hands of the King's Representative. After a lengthy assessment of the situation, the Rt. Hon. Sir Ronald Crawford Munro-Ferguson concluded with the statement — "That he had satisfied himself that the Leader who had the best prospect of securing unity among his followers, and being able to form a Government having those elements of permanence so essential to the conduct of affairs, was the Right Honourable W.M. Hughes". At that period the war in Europe had reached a most critical stage. The Germans had been massing for a spring offensive, which eventuated in an almost complete breakthrough to Paris and the French Channel Ports. The A.I.F. took a substantial part in checking the onslaught. In view of the gravity of the situation, Hughes did not hesitate in forming a Government. His first speech in Parliament commenced with the words "We must build ships, and more ships and still more ships". He returned to Europe during that critical spring and stayed to attend the protracted peace conference in 1919. His representation of Australia in the gathering of other allied leaders was a masterpiece of strategy and bargaining. His great services to Australia were recognised by a testimonial cheque for £25,000, presented to him at an enthusiastic meeting in Sydney in 1920.

It was in April, 1918 that the Australian Prime Minister and his staff embarked on R.M.S. *Niagara* for Europe via America. On their return voyage they left Devonport on the 11th July, 1919. This journey is not mentioned in the autobiographies or memoirs, though it must have been a most interesting experience. The vessel they travelled on was H.M.A.T. *Friedrichsruh*, a British built, ex-German ship then 15 years old. She had spent the war years alongside the quay in the Port of Bremen, and care and maintenance had been negligible. Her tonnage, 7,000 gross, did not make her a large vessel. She had tween deck holds, shelter deck and passenger accommodation for 50 people under somewhat spartan conditions. She had been named *Furst Bismarsk* after one of the country's national heroes. Before handing the ship over to the victors as a troopship, permission was sought and granted that the name be changed. The German authorities thought it improper that a ship named after the nation's greatest soldier and statesman should be used to carry victorious enemy troops back to their homeland. *Friedrichsruh* was the name of the Bismarck estate. A thousand Australian diggers under the command of Lt. Col. H.O. Caddy C.M.G. D.S.O. embarked at Devonport for the voyage home.

The Prime Minister and his staff shared what passenger accommodation there was with the senior officers. The troops had temporary amenities fitted in the 'tween decks. The ship was designed for a speed of 14 knots, but never attained this on her Australian trooping voyage. The journey to the Cape via Dakar was a long and weary one. She arrived at Capetown only by virtue of the trimmers sweeping out the bunkers, as the fuel consumption was beyond all expectations. Shortage of water was another difficulty but the biggest problems were in the stokehold. Engineers worked double shifts replacing boiler tubes, the South African coal was of doubtful quality, and the long haul across the Southern Ocean to Fremantle must have been a very weary one for the troops in the confines of the 'tween decks.

The long voyage would have provided a much needed rest for Australia's Prime Minister. To quote the poet "He had walked with Kings, yet kept the common touch". From the outset of his political career, social reform had been his main objective. He had always sought the other man's point of view and, with the end of the war, he also saw the end of an era, and a time for reconstruction. On this long voyage, with a thousand troops for company, men from all walks of life and of diverse views, William Morris Hughes who had done so many jobs, now become one of the world's great statesmen, would have without doubt utilised those weeks finding out by debate and query the sort of brave new world the returning Diggers wanted. *Friedrichsruh* arrived at Fremantle on August 24th. It was rumoured around the troop deck that, to achieve this, the boilers had to be bound together with hoop iron. Mr Hughes could not have been impressed by the ship's performance. She did not join the fleet of the Commonweath line. The Prime Minister continued his journey to the Eastern States by the recently opened Trans-Continental Railway. He was given a rousing reception at all stops en route and returned to Melbourne to take up the mammoth task of rebuilding Australia's economy.

The post-war period in Australia was, as in other parts of the world, one of trial and error. The ocean of politics, never placid, was in continuous turmoil. The Hughes Government was defeated on May 9th, 1923. On this occasion, William Morris Hughes tendered his resignation to the Governor-General and made the necessary advice regarding his successor, having been Australia's Prime Minister for almost 8 years. Lord Forster summoned Stanley Melbourne Bruce and requested him to form a Government. It is significant that the fortunes of the Commonwealth Line showed a sharp decline from May, 1923. In that year, the Commonwealth Line comprised just over 38% of Australasian tonnage. The fleet then comprised 3 "Australs", 10 ex-Germans, 6 D Class, 9 E Class, 2 "Dales" and the 5 "Bay" Ships. Four E Class ships had been sold to the Broken Hill Company. They were *Euwarra, Euroa, Eurimbla, Elouera.* They became *Iron Knob,* and *Iron Crown, Iron Master,* and *Iron Prince.* Competition on the Australian coastal trade had always been keen. With the completion of the East-West Railway, and the final link of the railway from Townsville to Cairns, thus joining all Queensland ports to Brisbane and Interstate rail systems, shipping competition intensified. A newcomer like the Commonwealth Line stood a poor chance of acquiring business. Coastal shipping companies such as the A.U.S.N. Co., Howard Smith, and the Adelaide S.S. Co. and several others, had been long established. They owned the wharves and other port facilities. Their ships had returned from war service and the owners were anxious to re-establish trade links and schedules. By 1925 the Government fleet was reduced to 15 ships. The Australs were no more, only 4 ex-German ships remained, *Booral, Boorara, Bulla* and *Carina.* Two "D" class, *Delungra* and *Dinoga,* two "E" Class, *Emita* and *Erriba,* the two "Dales" and last but not least the "Bay" ships. The year 1926 saw the fleet reduced to the 5 "Bay" ships and the two "Dales". The A.U.S.N. Co. had built up their fleet with *Emita, Enoggera, Echuca, Erriba, Eurelia* and *Eromanga.* With their new owners they traded under the names of *Milora, Mildura, Mareeba, Murada, Mungana* and *Maranoa.* Extra samson posts and derricks were fitted to these ships to speed up cargo handling and to enable 8 gangs of watersiders to be employed on each ship. Burns Philp & Co. took over *Eudunda* for their island trade and renamed her *Mangola*. The Broken Hill Co., with the ever expanding steel industry, made a further addition to their fleet with *Eugowra* renamed *Iron Warrior*. All these ships had been well maintained and were in practically new condition. All gave their owners many years of service with the exception of *Milora* ex *Emita* which, in 1934, became yet another victim of the notorious "rip" in Port Philip Bay. The wholesale disposal of these units of the fleet caused much concern to Mr Hughes. In the Federal Parliament, the Prime Minister, Mr Bruce, dismissed the whole concept of a Government Shipping Line as a "socialist venture". In typical Hughes logic, the founder of the Commonwealth Line pointed out it was no different to a Government owned Railway.

Since their arrival from England the 5 "Bay" ships had fulfilled their owners' requirements. The ships were identical, with a gross tonnage of 14,176 tons, net tonnage of 8,582, and a deadweight capacity of 12,620 tons. They sailed from the "Royal Group" of docks in London, and Brisbane was their terminal port in Australia. When fully loaded they drew 30 feet, their length was 530 feet 9 inches, breadth 68 feet 3 inches and a depth to the shelter deck of 43 feet 6 inches. They were twin screw ships, turbine driven at 90 revolutions per minute for a speed of 15 knots, on a daily oil consumption of 90 tons. The boilers could be converted to use coal, should the change be necessary. There was a total of 6 holds and hatchways, some for refrigeration cargo, and accommodation for 732 passengers. In common with other migrant ships of that period, additional temporary portable accommodation in the 'tween decks of the cargo holds was provided for single male migrants on the southbound voyage. For the return journey to London this was dismantled and the space filled with wool. The "Bay" ships had been fitted to carry 12 first class passengers, somewhat hopefully; the Government thought this would be used by high ranking public servants on their journeys to and from London. It was soon found that this type of official preferred the more glamorous ships of the P. & O. and Orient Lines to the confines of a small deckspace beneath the bridge deck of one of the "Bay" ships. Almost traditionally "Vice-Regals" travelled on the Blue Funnel Liners *Nestor* and *Ulysses*. These 14,646 ton passenger cargo liners travelled via Las Palmas and Capetown. They carried 120 first class passengers in solid comfort; being mainly cargo carriers they were steady ships. All passenger accommodation was in the superstructure with easy access to the open deck. The "Bay" ships always carried their full complement of passengers to Australia. The Migration Officials at Australia House made sure of this. Any surplus migrants were booked on the P. & O. Branch Line and the Aberdeen Line, whose ships travelled via the Cape. Ships of the Orient Line also carried migrants, calling at Naples to pick up those from Italy. The "Bay" ships called at Malta for passengers and loading and discharging of cargo. They were well patronized by passengers from Australia to the United Kingdom, being the only one class ship travelling via Suez at the third class fare rate which remained static at £38 sterling for almost 20 years, Brisbane to London via Ports. Retired Service Officers and others with regular but limited incomes found it cheaper to live on the "Bay" ships than at a seaside hotel. They also carried coastal passengers whilst in Australian waters — the fare rate being Fremantle to Brisbane £11.

To comply with the Australian Navigation Act crew quarters and victualling were of high standard, making competition difficult with ships manned under

British Board of Trade conditions. In spite of this the Line was plagued with labour troubles. In Australia each section of the crew had its own Union: Seamen's Union, Stewards and Pantrymen's Union, Cooks, Bakers etc. On the British ships, all seafarers, with the exception of the officers, belonged to the National Seamen and Firemen's Union, making negotiations so much easier. On the "Bay" ships delays were frequent. Some of the disputes were comical but the results for the Line were disastrous. Unlike the mailships of the P. & O. and Orient Lines which had a reserve of speed to make up on lost schedules, the 14 knot "Bays" had no such reserve. For the year 1926-27 the seven ships of the Commonwealth Line showed a loss of £189,905, but had the ships been signing on their crews in London this loss would have turned to a healthy profit. Each "Bay" ship had an annual wage bill of £204,987; under British manning this would have been £87,229. Less than half of the seagoing staff were domiciled in Australia. The remainder lived in Britain.

The Bruce-Page Government several times stated that the ships should be sold. The Opposition led by William Morris Hughes, denounced this in no uncertain terms. The Country Party section of the Government were also against disposing of the line, pointing out that should the line go out of existence there would be an immediate freight rise and it was better to pay the deficit on the Line's balance sheet, than to have the shipowners in the combine dictate their terms. The situation came to a climax on 27 December, 1927 — the day of the Regatta in Sydney Harbour — a colourful scene in the bright sunshine. T.S.S. *Moreton Bay* was at anchor, she was to be Flagship. A distinguished list of guests had been invited aboard the Flagship for lunch — the guests included the Governor-General, the Rt. Hon. John Lawrence, Baron Stonehaven, G.C.M.G., D.S.O., and the Prime Minister, Stanley Melbourne Bruce. As the guests arrived the stewards went ashore. They argued that they had just concluded a hard passage. They could find better things to do in Sydney than look after the V.I.P.'s Other sections of the crew supported the stewards and what should have been a pleasant day out for the visitors developed into a fiasco. A few days later the Government announced the line was to be sold.

William Morris Hughes rallied all his forces to oppose this. Even today it is a debatable point whether the line was sold or given away. Mr Hughes' forceful argument in the house was full of sound logic. Subsequent events proved the truth of this. He asked the Government to provide a direct operating subsidy. Sometime before, under pressure from the "Conference Lines", the Government had raised freight rates to the level of overseas companies. Of this Hughes said "with the adoption of uniform rates with conference lines, the Commonwealth Line ceased to be an effective restraint. This association was looked upon as a betrayal of all original concepts". Uniform rates removed the opposition to the sale from the Country Party section of the Government. Perhaps the strongest argument put up by Mr Hughes, and to which there was no reply, was that of defence. He pointed out that each of the "Bay" ships will carry and is intended to carry eight 6 inch guns and one 4 inch. *Fordsdale* and *Ferndale* were designed to carry seven 6 inch guns. As a comparison, H.M.A.S. *Sydney* which destroyed the *Emden* mounted eight 6 inch and four 3 pounders.

The original cost of the Commonwealth Line had been £15,000,000. Early in 1923 the fleet was reorganised and the value written down to £4,700,000. The original cost of the 5 "Bay" ships was £6,000,000. In spite of the charge by Mr

Hughes that the Government was selling Australia's auxiliary Navy, in 1928 the sale went through. The buyers were the "Kylsant Group".. This Group owned or managed many ships. The pattern of ownership was a complex one, Royal Mail Co., Pacific S.N. Co. and White Star Line all being part of this Group. In 1926 the ships of the Aberdeen Line, which had previously sailed from London to Brisbane, were transferred to Liverpool under the management of the White Star Line. The original owners of the Aberdeen Line were Geo. Thompson & Co. and had been taken over by Shaw Savill & Co. To this somewhat bizarre pattern of ownership were added the 5 "Bays" and the two "Dales". The sale terms were as follows — Price £1,900,000 on £250,000 deposit, followed by ten annual instalments of £165,000 with interest added. A proviso was made that the ships had to be kept on British or Australian Registry for 10 years. This clause was included to ensure they would not be bought and converted to war ships by a foreign power. The black hull colours of the seven ex-Commonwealth ships were altered to the Aberdeen green and from 1928 onwards they traded under the flag of the Aberdeen and Commonwealth Line. Perhaps the story of these ships should end at this juncture. Forty years were to pass before the Australian Merchant Navy Flag was to reappear on the Thames with the arrival there of the new Container ships.

The best summary I have seen on the passing of the Commonwealth Line was a *Times* Editorial: "The Australian experience showed the impossibility of a high cost wage economy successfully operating slow passenger ships in which crew costs are a large part of total voyage costs". The reorganised line consisted of the five Bay ships, *Fordsdale, Ferndale, Mataroa* (ex *Diogenes*) *Tamaroa* (ex *Sophocles*), *Horatius, Euripides, Demosthenes* and *Themistocles*.

The transition did not go smoothly. The Australian crews were to deliver the ships to England and be repatriated. More strikes, more delays occurred, and during the voyages passengers complained loud and long over the poor service by the crew, especially the catering section. *Jervis Bay* on her delivery voyage in June 1928 had some trouble with stowaways which made world headlines. A wireless message from the ship then in the region of the Cocos Islands asked for naval assistance to deal with eight desperate stowaways. The cruiser *Enterprise,* then at Colombo, was the nearest ship. The Navy asked for further details. *Jervis Bay* replied that "the stowaways were under hatches, under constant guard by volunteer passengers, mutiny and incendiarism attempted". This gave the Navy and the outside World the message that the crew were involved. After a further message asking for immediate assistance was received, a party of 20 marines were despatched aboard *H.M.S. Slavol*. The *Jervis Bay* was intercepted and the stowaways removed, eventually to serve a six month term in Colombo Jail. The crew had not been involved in the trouble, nor had they been particularly helpful in stopping it. All the world wondered how a large ship with a crew of nearly 200 had been endangered by eight stowaways. *Jervis Bay* was carrying 610 passengers at the time. Many of them were women and children. It was consideration for their welfare that caused the ship's master to seek naval assistance. Shortly after joining the Aberdeen Fleet *Ferndale* ran aground off the coast of North Africa and became a total loss. In 1929, the "Bay" ships vacated the London Docks and sailed from Southampton. In Britain seamen's wages were reduced from £9 per month to £8 per month, and the lines of idle ships increased. Assisted Migration was halted, causing the P. & O. to withdraw their nine "Branch" ships from the Australian Trade. Five of these were only eight years old but eventually the whole fleet was sold for scrap. The migration "close down" was a severe blow for the Aberdeen and Commonwealth Line. World depression had brought world travel almost to a standstill.

The year 1931 saw the shipping slump at its worst and the failure of the Kylsant Group, with a consequent default of payments to the Commonwealth Government. Lord Kylsant was tried and convicted for issuing a false prospectus for the Royal Mail Line section of the Group. His only crime was over-optimism; there were few optimists around in the year 1931. Once again the *Times* leader put the situation succinctly; of Lord Kylsant they wrote: "All who knew him, acquitted him of any desire to act criminally, and they laid the responsibility on the assumption of duties beyond the power of any individual to bear and on a certain financial recklessness and a belief in the future which events showed was unjustified. Lord Kylsant bore his trial with great dignity and cast no blame on any colleagues". After serving 12 months imprisonment Lord Kylsant left the world of high finance and retired to Wales.

The Group was broken up and the six ex-Australian ships were sold for £500,000. The name of the Line was retained with the addition of the word Limited. Capital was provided by Shaw Savill and the P. & O. Line in equal parts and vested in a holding company to be known as the Aberdeen and Commonwealth Line Ltd. This was placed under the management of Shaw Savill. *Demosthenes* built at Belfast in 1912 was scrapped. *Euripides* built in 1915 was renamed *Akaroa* and placed on the New Zealand service. *Esperance Bay* was also diverted to New Zealand and renamed *Arawa*. *Esperance Bay* had always been a popular ship under the command of Captain McKenzie, who took over command of *Hobsons Bay*, which was promptly renamed *Esperance Bay*, thus preserving the alliance of a popular ship and popular Captain. From the days of the East Indiamen it was always the practice to couple the name of the captain with that of the ship in sailing lists and advertisements and the discerning traveller would make his choice on the captain's reputation. This form of advertising was not resumed after the Second World War. The Aberdeen and Commonwealth Line had great success with *Akaroa* ex *Euripides* converted into a one class ship for 200 passengers. She was formerly two class for 600 passengers. The passenger space surplus to requirements was modified for cargo. Sailing from Southampton the 100 day trip to and from New Zealand was advertised at £112. This included living aboard during the month the ship was in New Zealand waters. *Arawa* ex *Esperance Bay* received similar treatment and also became a popular cruise ship. The travelling public of the 30's were no longer satisfied with canvas swimming pools and inside cabins. The four remaining Bay ships were refitted to give passengers the comforts which the new fleet of the P. & O. Strath ships were providing. The Orient Line's *Orion* built at the same time also had many additional built-in features to get their share of the tourist trade.

Unemployment figures for British seamen in 1930 were 30%. This figure was maintained until Italy's Abyssinian adventure but in 1939 was still 20%. There were no serious industrial troubles during this period. Very few deserted from the ships which shipowners managed to keep in service. By 1935 Germany had a fleet of passenger and cargo ships far more modern than those of her former enemies. Under the terms of the German surrender agreement all merchant ships over

1,600 tons and half of the ships between 1,000 and 1,600 tons were confiscated. This would leave Germany with ships only suitable for the Baltic Trade. The reparation ships sailing under flags of the allies could not compete with the fast and well designed ships of the post-war German Merchant Navy. Other provisos of the peace terms were the completion and surrender of two thirds of the shipping tonnage under construction in 1918. Germany was also required to compensate shipowners for all shipping destroyed during the war. The currency collapse of 1920 saw shipowners receiving their compensation in worthless paper. With the outbreak of war in 1939 all the 5 "Bay" ships were commandeered – *Arawa* and *Jervis Bay* as armed merchant cruisers, with pig iron ballast in their lower holds and the remainder of the cargo spaces filled with empty oil drums. *Largs Bay, Moreton Bay,* and *Esperance Bay* all saw service in the various theatres of war. The epic story of the *Jervis Bay* against overwhelming odds on the afternoon of 5 November, 1940 has earned a place in the annals of seawarfare and is too well known to add to this story. I should imagine William Morris Hughes was indeed a proud man when news of the action came through, an action which left the name *Jervis Bay* engraved forever in history.

The remaining "Bay" ships survived the war. *Largs Bay* was badly damaged by a mine near Naples on January 2nd, 1944. All the armed merchant cruisers had been converted to troopers and assault ships by then, after *Rawalpindi, Jervis Bay* and others had paid the price of Admiralty. It was realised that with their lofty superstructures and low speed they were no match for the enemy ships of recent construction. At the end of the Second World War the "Bay" ships once again took an active part in Australia's post war migration program. *Arawa* ex *Esperance Bay* went to the breakers in 1955. *Esperance Bay* ex *Hobsons Bay* followed a few weeks later. *Moreton Bay* sailed on into 1957 then to the scrap yards. The last of the Bay ships, *Largs Bay's* final voyage was also made in 1957. The length of time of this voyage would compare with that of the sailing ships of the last century. A continuous run of engine and boiler mishaps during the voyage round the Cape, and lengthy stays for temporary repairs added weeks to the voyage. The closing of the Suez Canal had caused a "Bay" ship to be routed round the Cape for the first time. As an anti-climax to the voyage, "Largs Bay" anchored in the Solent before proceeding to Southampton. It appears the passengers, knowing the ship was destined to go to the breakers, laid claim to many moveable parts of the ship's fittings. The Company provided a tug to send a party of Police to the ship to search the passengers' luggage and recover the property, and this having been done, the last of the "Bay" ships ended her final voyage. Another remarkable but unglamorous ship of the Aberdeen and Commonwealth Line also went to the shipbreakers at Dalmuir on August 24th 1947 – *Themistocles,* launched at Harlands and Wolffs' Belfast Yard on September 22nd 1910. The ship carried 100 first class, 250 third class and 240 single male migrant passengers in the 'tween decks of No. 1 & 2 holds. Apart from trooping service in the two World Wars, her entire working life was spent on the London (later Liverpool) to Brisbane passenger and cargo service, calling at Teneriffe and Capetown, and making her Australian landfall at Albany. This 11,250 ton ship remained a coal burner all her long and busy life.

What of the other ships of the Commonwealth Government Shipping Line? In the early 1930's I saw a ship bearing the name *"Dimitrios N. Rallas"* ex *Liberta* ex *Australfield* ex *Vermont* loading wheat at Geelong. A friend who had the misfortune to be travelling as a P.O.W. in the hold of a Japanese ship in 1942, recalls seeing the name "Strath" on the hatch coamings and on a rare visit to the Upper Deck saw the builders' plate below the bridge — Duncan & Co. Glasgow 1906, so it would appear that *Miho Maru* ex *Australpool* ex *Strathairly* completed at least 36 years of service for her various owners. All the Australian built ships taken over by coastal shipping companies proved a credit to their builders. *Mareeba* ex *Echuca* fell a victim to the German raider *Kormoran* in the Indian Ocean. *Mareeba* left Fremantle loaded with flour consigned to Colombo on 13 May, 1941.

The architect and founder of the Australian Commonwealth Line, Mr William Morris Hughes, died on 28 October 1952, completing 58 years of parliamentary service. On 15 October 1953, in the crypt of St. Paul's Cathedral, a memorial plaque was unveiled to honour this great statesman. The Duke of Gloucester performed the ceremony. A few minutes walk from there, the Thames flows down to the sea a murky stream, but it has been rightly described as liquid history. As the memory of W.M. Hughes was so honoured in St. Paul's Cathedral one can reflect and look back to that autumn day in 1884 when Hughes, fired with the spirit of adventure, journeyed down the Thames to join *The Duke of Westminster*.

Chapter 3

THE "AUSTRAL SHIPS"

The first group of ships to be registered under the ownership of the Commonwealth Line were the ex "Strath" ships, 10 in number, and almost the entire fleet of Burrell & Sons of Glasgow. Their dimensions and tonnages were somewhat similar, but they were not sister ships and varied in the design of their superstructures.

A gross tonnage of 4,300 tons, nett tonnage of 2,900, length 375 feet, breadth 52 feet and a depth of 25 feet, they were not a triumph of naval architecture, just floating warehouses built to carry the maximum amount of cargo at the cheapest possible cost.

Strathesk, built in 1909 by the Greenoch and Grangemouth Shipyard on the Clyde, became *Australbrook* her port of registry Melbourne. During the twelve months from October, 1916 to October, 1917, twenty-three voyages were made by the Austral ships from Australia to United Kingdom ports, in each case with a capacity cargo. *Australbrook's* first cargo was copra, zinc concentrates and wheat. Even the forepeaks, lazarets, and other available spaces were loaded with cordage, binder-twine and honey. From October 1917 to 1 August 1918, nineteen voyages were made by the Australs from Australia, fourteen to the United Kingdom and five to the Pacific Coast ports of the American continent, the main cargoes being wheat and flour. Each of the ex "Strath" ships had a dead weight capacity of 7,180 tons. In 1914 the freight on wheat Australia to British or Continental ports was 25/- per ton. By 1917, this had risen to £15 per ton. The Australian Commonwealth Line ships carried wheat for £6 per ton. Even at this rate, the ships showed a handsome profit.

Bunker coal in Australia was obtainable at a low price. Screened Waratah coal delivered alongside ship in Sydney was quoted at 17s.0¾d. per ton in April, 1917; under the same date West Wallsend screened coal could be procured at Newcastle, N.S.W. for 11s.9d. per ton. A ship such as *Australbrook* would consume about 32 tons per day. Her post war voyages were also quite profitable. On her journey from Britain with general cargo for Fremantle, Adelaide, Melbourne, Sydney and Brisbane, *Australbrook* left Capetown on 1 October, 1920 and completed discharging at Brisbane on 15 November. She then loaded timber for discharge at Sydney, where she spent some days undergoing repairs, then loaded general cargo for the United Kingdom. Leaving Sydney on 3 December, 1920 she then proceeded to Adelaide to load wool and general cargo for New York and Boston, via Panama; the ship also loaded cargo for Hull and London. She left Adelaide for Newcastle, N.S.W. on 30 December, 1920. *Australbrook* filled her bunkers at Newcastle for the long lonely haul across the Pacific on 8 January 1921 and finished her voyage at London on 7 April, 1921. This round the world voyage of seven months duration, loading and discharging at so many ports, was quite a creditable performance. She continued her voyages until 1924, followed by a period of "laying up", and passed into Japanese ownership early in 1926, to sail under the name of *Uga Maru*.

Strathendrick, built in 1907 by Napier and Miller of Glasgow, was one of the first of the "Strath" ships to arrive in Australia. She took the name *Australdale* with Brisbane as her port of registry. Her career with the Commonwealth Line was just a brief one. She was torpedoed and sunk on 5 October, 1917 whilst outward bound from Bristol Channel ports on her way to Australia. One man was killed by the explosion; the rest of the crew took to the boats — one boat with 24 survivors on board was never seen again. *Australdale* went down within minutes of the torpedo striking just forward of the stokehold.

Strathgarry, also built in 1907 by the Hamilton Shipbuilding Co. of Glasgow, changed her name to *Australbush* registered at Adelaide. She took part in moving Australia's wheat crop, then her epitaph appeared on the fleet list "lost through enemy action". She was torpedoed and sunk on 15 November 1917 in the Channel approaches near Portsmouth. Her sinking would not be an important event in the year 1917 when the U Boats appeared to have supremacy on the seaways leading to Europe. She was just another salt stained tramp steamer, unglamorous, and her only protection against the submarine peril was a coat of camouflage paint. The British Government compensated shipowners for all sinkings and damage by the enemy under a war risk clause. Whether this applied to *Australdale* and *Australbush* is not clear; however, the Commonwealth Line received compensation from some source. In Appendix "B" of the Financial Statement showing the position of the Commonwealth Fleet at 30 June 1923, amongst "Profits, recoveries and present market values" one item: is "Amounts recovered on account of vessels lost at sea £791,897".

Strathleven, another product of the Hamilton ship building yard on the River Clyde, was also built in 1907. This seems to have been a year of expansion for "Tramp" tonnage — it was also a time of re-armament and the building of huge navies. Britain's naval bases were scattered throughout the world, from the Falkland Islands to the China Station. Warships were, and still are, extravagant on fuel; in 1907 coal was the only fuel for surface ships, usually Welsh smokeless anthracite. The "Strath" ships, and many more like them, carried coal to bunkering stations in all continents, returning with cargoes of grain, cotton, iron ore, concentrates, sugar or esparto grass. *Strathleven* joined the Commonwealth Line fleet as *Australcrag,* Melbourne being her port of registry. Like the other "Australs", wheat became her main cargo and she continued in this trade after the war. On 16 November 1920, *Australcrag* filled her bunkers at Newcastle, N.S.W. and sailed to Wallaroo to load a full cargo of wheat for the continent. She had just completed a voyage from the U.K. with general cargo, completing her discharge at Brisbane on 10 November, 1920. Her holds full of South Australian grain, *Australcrag* sailed to Albany, Western Australia for bunkering, leaving there on 10 December 1920 and arrived at Durban twenty days later. From there she sailed to Hull, arriving on 8 February 1921. *Australcrag* had been scheduled to load general cargo at Antwerp, Hull, Middlesborough and London for the capital city ports of Australia. Due to industrial troubles the ship crossed the channel to load a full cargo for New Zealand, arriving at Ghent on 1 March 1921. Two weeks were spent loading in the Belgian port. *Australcrag* then sailed for Panama, arriving on 9 April, and departing the next day for Auckland and New Plymouth. Her trans-Pacific passage was a lengthy one — she arrived at Auckland on 11 May 1921.

The year 1921 was a difficult one for coal burning ships sailing from Europe. The German coalfields were in low production due to the post-war political situation. A series of strikes in the coalfields of Britain made good bunker coal a vary scarce commodity. The coal that was available was of poor quality and more suitable for a slag heap than a ship's bunkers, American coal was available at Norfolk, Virginia, and was known among the stokers and trimmers as "Yankee slack". In spite of adjustments to the firebars, much of this slack found its way into the ashpits. Poor steaming did not make a happy ship. The deck officers made their noon sightings and submitted them to the Captain, who would pass caustic comments to the chief engineer, who in turn would urge the watch-keeping engineers to pay more frequent visits to the stokehold instead of reading Edgar Wallace novels in the engine room.The engineers would curse the stokers, the stokers would curse the trimmers, and the trimmers would curse the coal. So the time taken by the "Australs" on their round the world voyages, with bunker coal a perpetual problem, was quite reasonable. There were no ocean greyhounds in the tramp fleets. *Australcrag* remained in the Commonwealth Line until the passing of the Commonwealth Shipping Act of 1923, when the line was placed under the control of a Board of Directors. *Australcrag* was then sold to Japanese shipping interests to continue trading under the name of *Misaka Maru* and the flag of the rising sun.

Strathdee, another steamer of 1907 vintage and a product of the Clydeside Shipbuilders, R. Duncan & Co., took the name *Australrange*. She was registered at Sydney. She made several war-time wheat-laden voyages, and played her part in keeping Britain and her allies from starvation. Her post war voyages followed the route for the other "Australs" already detailed. It would appear that at that period of history Australia had to import sugar. *Australrange* arrived at the Irish port of Limerick with a full cargo of wheat on 21 December 1920. The ship had loaded her cargo at Port Pirie and Port Augusta, leaving the latter port on 10 October. Her stay in Australia had been quite a long one on this occasion. *Australrange* had arrived in Sydney on 3 July 1920 with a full cargo of sulphur, having left Panama on 31 May. After discharging her wheat cargo, this hardworking Australian tramp steamer sailed over to Penarth in South Wales to refill her bunkers for the long voyage home via Neuvitas in Cuba. This little known port is on the North Coast of the island. The "Australs" were versatile and capable of loading and discharinging at the most outlandish places where no assistance from tugs was available and the pilot was often a local fisherman.

Australrange made the voyage to Cuba "in ballast" and arrived on 2 March. The four thousand mile voyage took 21 days. In "ballast trim" the early part of the voyage to the region of the Azores and the "Flying Fish" weather could have been quite an ordeal for the ship and her crew at that time of the year.

It was not at all unusual for ships to have their engines full ahead to remain in the same part of the Atlantic Ocean for several days. The "Austral" type of ship would have no automatic device to stop the propeller racing as the vessels pitching and rolling brought it clear of the sea into the air. The engineer on watch could minimise this to a certain extent by anticipating the ship's movements and controlling the steam accordingly. The Cuban stevedores must have been good toilers, for they had the ballast discharged and a full cargo of sugar loaded in 15 days.

Australrange cleared Balboa for Sydney, arriving there on 28 April 1921, yet another of the "Australs" to circumnavigate the world. After a period of "coasting", it was found that too many ships were competing for the cargo available and *Australrange* became another ship of the Japanese Mercantile Marine under the name of *Ishikari Maru*.

Strathairly, was another of the products of the Clydeside shipbuilders, R. Duncan & Co. The three cylinder engine of 367 N.H.P. was made by David Rowan & Co. of Glasgow. The "Strath" ships, whilst under the management of Burrell & Son, appeared to be individually owned and even some of the single ships were divided into shares of one sixty-fourth. This peculiar system is said to have been continued from ancient times, originating in the Norse Longships of Leif Ericson a thousand years ago. *Strathairly* was built in 1906 for Strathairly Steamship Co. and was their one and only ship. She was taken over by the Commonwealth Government on June 13, 1916 when still under Admiralty requisition. On completing this assignment, *Strathairly* became *Australpool,* registered at Fremantle. A full cargo was loaded and *Australpool* departed for Melbourne via New York and Papeete. She sailed up the Yarra early in January, 1917. No time was wasted in getting her round to the wheat ports and *Australpool* was back in the war zone by April. She was one of the few "Australs" to do Mediterranean voyages and passed through the Suez Canal on October 4, 1920 with a full cargo of flour for famine relief in Greece. From there she sailed to ports in the United Kingdom to load general cargo for Australian ports via Capetown. She left London, her final loading port, on 5 December 1920. *Australpool* had the distinction of being one of the few merchant ships to visit Westernport Bay in Victoria. She discharged naval stores there in mid-July, 1920. At that time Flinders Naval Base, later to become the Australian Navy's main training establishment, was in the course of erection. Now knows as *H.M.A.S. Cerberus,* with its green lawns, trees and hedges, it stands as an oasis among the desolate tidal swamps of Westernport Bay. In 1920 there were no wharf facilities or amenities of any kind, so *Australpool* would have had to anchor well offshore and discharge her cargo into lighters. The years 1920 and 1921 seemed to be the peak of the post war shipping boom. After that the shipping lists show an ever increasing number of "ballast" voyages, an item expensive to load and discharge and which paid no freight. In 1924 *Australpool* passed into the ownership of the Matzuaka Kizen and sailed on as *Miho Maru,* registered at Fuchu.

Strathbeg , another of the 1907 Clyde built ships from the yards of W. Hamilton of Glasgow, was, like the other "Straths", listed 100, A1, Lloyds' highest classification, at the time of her purchase by the Australian Government. Sydney became her port of registration and her new name *Australmount.* Post war voyages took her around the world, one voyage including the port of Manchester. The ship left Fremantle on 27 September 1920 with a full cargo of wool, wheat and general cargo for Liverpool and Manchester. She arrived at Liverpool on 3 December and made the 36 mile passage up the canal to Manchester a few days later. No outward cargo was offering around the Mersey ports, so *Australmount* proceeded to the bunkering port of Barry in South Wales. In addition to filling her bunkers *Australmount* also loaded a full cargo of coal for for Azores. This put the ship well on her way to Cuba where a cargo of sugar was waiting for shipment to Australia. The crew would be fully employed on the run from the Azores to the West Indies, cleaning up the holds ready for the sugar cargo. Once again loading in Cuba took only a few days. *Australmount* passed through the Panama Canal on her way to Sydney on 17 February 1921 and arrived there on 14 March. A short period for refit and *Australmount* left for another round world voyage, this time under charter to the Australian Wheat Board to Plymouth for orders. On returning to Australia at the end of the voyage, the ship had a period of laying up. Queensland's sugar production was increasing and imports from overseas were drastically curtailed. This meant a twelve thousand mile "ballast" voyage after the "Australs" had delivered their wheat and so *Australmount* ex *Strathbeg* journeyed north to take part in the Burma Rice Trade as *Asaka Maru.*

Strathspey built in 1906, by the Grangemouth and Greenock Dockyard on the Clyde, joined the Australian Government fleet in 1916, was re-named *Australpeak* and registered at Brisbane. Practically all the wartime wheat cargoes were loaded in Victoria and South Australia. *Australpeak* made Brisbane her terminal port in Australia when carrying general cargo from Europe. Between wheat shipments the ship was employed on the Australian coastal trade. Typical of the post war voyages of the "Australs", *Australpeak* arrived at Melbourne on 22 November 1920 and dischargd a load of timber and pig iron loaded at Newcastle a few days previously. Some repairs were carried out by the Williamstown Dockyard and the ship was then despatched to Wallaroo to load a full cargo of wheat for Hamburg. Ten days were spent at the Spencer Gulf wheatport, and *Australpeak* left for Capetown on 23 December 1920. She arrived at Hamburg on 28 February 1921. A cargo of wheat would have been a welcome sight to the people of Hamburg at that time. The situation was one of chaos — responsible Government had collapsed and, with it, the monetary system. In Britain thousand mark notes were being used as wallpaper, being cheaper than the genuine article. Germany was an occupied country, reeling under the effects of reparations and other conditions of the peace treaty of Versailles. How Australia was paid for the wheat is not on record, but it would appear to have been part of a general famine relief programme. On discharge of her cargo *Australpeak* was scheduled to call at Newport, Liverpool and Glasgow for loading for Fremantle, Adelaide, Melbourne, Sydney and Brisbane. This was not to be. The post war shipping boom was already showing signs of collapse. After steaming to various British ports *Australpeak* arrived at Southampton on 2 April 1921. From there she left for Fremantle with only ballast in her holds and arrived in Australia on 2 June. *Australpeak* carried out a few charter voyages for the Broken Hill Co., then spent some months "laid up" in Sydney Harbour before being sold. This ship was the only "Austral" to carry on sailing under the British flag. She was bought by the Carspey Steamship Co., under the management of Wm. Stewart & Co., who registered her at the port of London and gave her the name *Carspey*.

Strathavon, built in 1907, another product of the Grangemouth and Greenock shipyard, joined the Commonwealth fleet as *Australford,* and Adelaide was selected as her port of registry. She seemed to be more fortunate in procuring cargoes than the other "Australs". I have no record of any ballast voyages in her history. Having discharged a wheat cargo at British ports in August 1920, *Australford* delivered a coal cargo to the British West Indies, and arrived at the Texan City of Port Arthur on 22 October to load case oil. As other Australian ships also loaded this type of cargo, a few lines of explanation may be necessary for those who in these days of bulk handling may not know what case oil was. Kerosene, lubricating oil and benzine, now always referred to as petroleum products, were made up in four gallon tins and packed two tins to a case. Both the tins and cases were well made, the latter of dressed pine. Each case weighed eighty pounds and could be carried on pack saddles of horses and camels. Sailing ships carried case oil to China, returning with the tea crop. The empty tins and cases were much sought after and put to various uses. In Queensland during the migration boom of the early 1920's the New Settlers' League issued a booklet with diagrams for furnishing a home using kerosene tins and cases; cut at an angle one tin would make a double sink, a dozen cases and a few yards of cretonne would make a lounge suite. A case oil cargo was a popular one with both shipowners and ships' crews. It stowed well, did not shift in heavy seas and could be handled by the ship's own cargo gear. Brisbane was the first Australian port of call for *Australford* and her cargo of case oil. She arrived on Christmas Eve 1920, and did not leave until 31 January 1921. The holidays would have caused some delay and the wet season may have also hindered discharge of the cargo. *Australford* continued to Sydney, Beauty Point (Tasmania), Adelaide and Melbourne, unloading her case oil cargo at each of these ports. The month's delay in the vessel's unloading had not been anticipated. When sailing from Panama on November, 18 1920, the Commonwealth Line announced *Australford* would complete unloading at Melbourne on 21 January 1921. When the ship did eventually reach Melbourne, she underwent repairs in dry dock, then sailed to Newcastle, N.S.W. for bunkers; having filled these to capacity, *Australford* was ready for her next assignment. She arrived at Portland, Victoria on 6 March 1921, commenced loading next day, and sailed for Durban a week later. *Australford* replenished her bunkers at Durban on 10 April and proceeded to Antwerp to discharge her full cargo of wheat. Fortune smiled upon this ship of the Commonwealth Line. Cargo for Australia was awaiting shipment on the Antwerp wharves. Taking this into her holds, *Australford* crossed over to Hull, arriving on 4 June. Loading further cargo at Middlesborough and London, she sailed for Adelaide, Melbourne and Sydney on 18 June 1921. On discharging in Sydney no work was available and the ship anchored in Watsons Bay. Freights on wheat cargoes showed quite a dramatic drop from 1922 onwards, in 1930 reaching a low of 30s. per ton. from Australia to Europe. No Australian ship could have operated without heavy loss at these rates, with no prospects of a return cargo. As the months went by and the costs of laying up mounted, *Australford* weighed anchor and joined Japan's ever-expanding fleet as *Unyo Maru*.

The last of the ten "Strath" ships *Strathord*, built in 1906 on the busy banks of the Clyde by the Grangemouth and Greenock Shipyard, took over the name *Australglen* on joining the fleet of the Commonwealth Line. To re-assure Tasmanians that they were not forgotten, *Australglen* was registered at Hobart. She came through the War unscathed and took her place with the other "Australs" competing on an ever-declining freight market. Ballast voyaging is mentioned frequently on her list of sailings. She left Sydney 29 September 1920 in ballast for Port Augusta to take on a part cargo of wheat, and completed loading at Wallaroo. This was a charter voyage, the wheat to be unloaded at Belfast. *Australglen* departed from Wallaroo on 4 November and arrived at Belfast on 6 January 1921, a slow voyage of over two months, followed by a ballast voyage to Barry, South Wales for coaling. *Australglen* sailed from the Bristol Channel on 21 February 1921 bound for Cuba to load sugar for Sydney. Her destination, Paloalto, does not appear on any of the present day maps of Cuba. The Harbour could have silted up and the settlement become just another forgotten port, or the name could have been changed in the various political upheavals which have taken place over the last twenty years. However. *Australglen* found her way there, arriving on 14 March, a leisurely voyage of 4,000 miles in three weeks. The loading of a full cargo of bagged sugar was completed in two weeks. *Australglen* negotiated the Panama Canal, cleared Balboa on 3 April and arrived in Sydney on 11 May 1921, just over 6 months after leaving South Australia.

The voyage would have been quite a profitable one, but without the return sugar cargo from Cuba the balance sheet would have been different. For many years Australia had been self sufficient in the production of sugar. In addition to this, there was quite a healthy export trade. The 1914 War, with its manpower problems, caused a sharp decline in the acreage of canefields in Queensland and northern New South Wales. In 1915 the Commonwealth Government placed an export embargo on sugar. In 1920 production had risen to 182,000 tons. By 1923 Australia's annual sugar crop showed a rapid rise with a surplus for export of 74,000 tons. Again, the Government moved and placed an embargo on all imports of sugar. As West Indies sugar had been among the few cargoes offering for the homeward bound Australian wheatships, a re-assessment of the Australian Commonwealth Line had to be made. This resulted in *Australglen* changing her name to *Ginro Maru*.

I have concentrated on the voyages of the "Strath" ships and the cargoes carried by them as typical of the war-time and immediate post war assignments of the ships of the Australian Commonwealth Line. The five remaining ships of the 1916 London purchase varied in age from *Dalton Hall* of 1899 to *Ardangorm* of 1915. They are listed as follows:-

Kirkoswald built 1912 by A. McMillan of Dumbarton. 4,151 tons gross. 2,476 net. Re-named *Australmead* of Melbourne.

Ardanmhor built 1907 by H. & W. Henderson, Glasgow. 4,438 tons gross, 2,829 net, to become *Australplain* of Fremantle.

9. s.s. *Australpeak* ex *Strathspey*.

10. s.s. *Australbrook* ex *Strathesk*.

11. s.s. *Australpool* ex *Strathairly*.

12. s.s. *Australport* ex *Ardongorm*.

E CLASS SHIPS

13. s.s. *Echuca* being launched at Maryborough, Queensland 16 July 1921.

14. s.s. *Echuca* raising steam for trails at fitting out wharf of Walkers Limited, Maryborough, Queensland.

15. s.s. *Echuca* proceeding down Mary River to undergo builder's trials in Hervey Bay.

16. s.s. *Mareeba*, A.U.S.N. Company, ex s.s. *Echuca*, Australian Commonwealth Line.

17. Scuttling of s.s. *Milora*, formerly s.s. *Emita*, Australian Commonwealth Line. Stranded on Rondella Reef, 21 September 1934 with a full cargo of coal from Newcastle, New South Wales. Refloated two days later. Hull damaged beyond economic repair. After removal of fittings towed out beyond Point Lonsdale and scuttled.

DALE SHIPS

18. s.s. *Ferndale*.

19. T.s.s. *Fordsdale*. Note the catwalk around the funnel which was to facilitate the removal of the top half of the funnel, which was left ashore at Eastham before entering the Manchester ship canal. The Dale ships were also fitted with telescopic masts for the negotiation of the ship canal.

BAY SHIPS

20. s.s. *Jervis Bay*. Aberdeen and Commonwealth Line. One class service between England and Australia via Suez.

21. R.M.S. *Arawa* ex *Esperance Bay I*. 14,500 tons. Shaw Saville Line to New Zealand.

VARIOUS SHIPS

22. s.s. *Themistocles.* Aberdeen Line.

23. T.S.S. *Indarra*, A.U.S.N. Co., under Orient Line colours 1921.

Ardangorm built 1915 by Napier & Miller of Glasgow. 3,579 tons gross, 2,289 net. Re-named *Australport* of Port Adelaide.

Dalton Hall built 1899 by Furness Withy & Co. of West Hartlepool, 3,534,tons gross. Re-named *Australstream* of Sydney.

Vermont built 1900 by Barclay, Curle & Co., Glasgow. 4,271 tons gross. Re-named *Australfield* of Hobart.

Australmead had a dead weight cargo capacity of 7,740 tons. Apart from being of modern build, she was the largest ship of the 15 which made up the 1916 London purchase. Her post war voyages included a cargo of wheat for Egypt, which arrived at Port Soudan on 1 January 1921. The bagged wheat was loaded at Fremantle in November 1920. *Australmead* made the return voyage to Australia in ballast via Colombo. She sailed again with a general cargo for London, Swansea, Liverpool and Glasgow, leaving Fremantle 8 April, 1921.

Australplain managed to do several round the world voyages: wheat to Europe, ballast to Cuba, and sugar from Cuba to Sydney. On these voyages she was on charter to the Australian Wheat Board.

Australport appears to have made Middlesborough her main British loading port on conclusion of her wheat voyages. The Yorkshire port is Britain's main outlet for steel products and perhaps there were special features about *Australport,* such as large hatchways, which made the ship suitable for the carrying of structural steel. *Australport* arrived at Townsville on 16 June 1920 with a full cargo of case oil from New York. The entire shipment was consigned to Queensland, completing discharge at Rockhampton and Brisbane. Rockhampton is a town on the Tropic of Capricorn, 40 miles of navigation from Keppel Bay up the winding reaches of the Fitzroy River. *Australport* must have been one of the largest ships ever to negotiate the passage of the Fitzroy River as the river port usually catered for coastal ships. Rockhampton is no longer a port; siltation and other problems caused the closing some years ago. Port Alma, a deepwater harbour on the delta of the Fitzroy River, now handles the sea-borne imports and exports for Rockhampton and its hinterland.

Australfield only stayed in the fleet for a few months after completing her war-time assignments. She was then sold to a Balkan syndicate and sailed on under the name of *Liberta.*

Australstream does not appear on any of the 1920 sailing lists or amongst the vessels laid up for various reasons. This Durham built tramp steamer later sailed as *General Degoute* under foreign ownership, probably Greek.

To summarize the story of the Austral ships and their failure to compete in the post war years of reconstruction: many startling changes had taken place in the world since these ships were launched into the murky waters of the Clyde. Coal, a tramp ship's basic cargo, was on the way out as a fuel — oil and hydro-electricity were taking its place. The U.S.A. and Canada had increased their wheat production and bulk handling facilities. The main British ports also installed suction methods of unloading the bulk wheat ships. It was only in the smaller ports of Ipshwick, Dublin and a few other places that bagged wheat could be handled. The Atlantic seaboard of the American continent was only 10 days steaming from Britain, compared with the 40 days passage to the Australian wheat centres. Even the express passenger ships of the White Star Line, *Baltic, Celtic, Cedric, Adriatic,* etc. carried bulk wheat in their lower holds on their crossings from New York and Boston to Liverpool. Wheat was quickly loaded and unloaded so did not interfere with sailing schedules. By 1927 only the occasional tramp steamer which, after delivering a cargo of cement or sulphur to the Antipodes, would load a cargo of Australian wheat and then only from the silos in bulk form. The price of wheat was low on world markets and only the cheapest freights for Australian grain could land the wheat at a competitive price.

One bright spot in the gloomy picture was the new lease of life this situation gave to the remaining sailing ships in the world. A sailing ship has the advantage that all space below deck can be used for cargo. A great deal of Australia's wheat was grown around Spencer Gulf in South Australia. Loading and other harbour facilities were poor at the ports there. Ships would be several weeks loading a cargo of 5 or 6 thousand bags of wheat, each one weighing 180 pounds. Port Augusta, Port Garmein and Port Lincoln were only one-jetty ports. Port Victoria and Port Broughton had no wharves. Ships loading remained at anchor and the wheat was brought out to them in sailing ketches. Captain Erikson bought more than a dozen large sailing ships, most of them ex-German nitrate carriers; as these ships were unwanted elsewhere the Finnish shipowner was able to buy them very cheaply and, by using every possible economy, was able to move the bulk of the South Australian wheat crop to Europe. Many of his crews were indentured, receiving only a token wage and paying for the privilege of working the ship. Certain exclusive pilotage services such as Liverpool Bay and the Hoogly required a certificate of one year's service in square riggers, in addition to the normal qualifications from would-be entrants into their services.

So berths on the Erikson ships were sought after by young seamen with an eye to the future. Only on rare occasions would cargo be found for the south-bound voyage to the wheatports of Australia; sand, rubble or shingle ballast gave the ships the necessary trim to sail through the southern oceans and the roaring forties. This was dumped by manpower at a designated part of Spencer Gulf. Captain Erikson managed to keep his fleet going until the second World War. Each ship made one voyage a year, the remaining time being spent at the anchorage at Mariehamn in the Finnish Aaland Islands. No insurance was carried on the ships; this and other economies enabled the vessels to pay their way. Captain Erikson, dedicated to sail, did not make a fortune from his fleet.

In 1920, Canada had also accumulated quite a large fleet of tramp steamers, of similar tonnage to the "Australs", their names were prefixed "Canadian": *Canadian Trooper, Canadian Fisher,* etc. Scores of these ships were laid up around the Gulf of St. Lawrence and eventually bought by Aristotle Onassis at scrap prices to sail under the Greek flag and make a fortune for their enterprising owner. Stark facts and world economics brought about the sale of the "Australs". Even if the crews had been of angelic temperament and worked for nothing, the sale of the "Australs" may have only been delayed for a while. Coal-burning tramp steamers, like the sailing ships before them, were becoming a thing of the past.

The generalisation that crew trouble caused the demise of the Commonwealth Line has only a small element of truth in it. The delayed voyages had many causes. Instances are found in news columns of those years. Two well known Australian traders, the White Star Line *Ceramic,* and Aberdeen Line *Euripides,* arrived at Plymouth on 1 January 1920. After disembarking passengers they proceeded to the Thames to discharge their refrigerated cargoes, but even with a top priority, these valuable ships were anchored off Southend for three weeks waiting for a berth at the congested London Docks. It was early in March before their much needed cargoes were unloaded. Post-war congestion and the influenza epidemic caused these delays. Tramp steamers like the "Australs" would have only a low priority for dockside labour. Australia has only a short history, but the Scottish built "Austral" ships and those who went down to the sea in them should become part of that history.

Chapter 4

THE GERMAN SHIPS

The German ships which comprised a large section of the Australian Commonwealth Shipping Line were registered in London, with the exception of *Parattah*, registered in Sydney. The history of the ships from the time of their requisition in 1914 is rather confusing. Some were under the control of the British Board of Trade, others were manned with crews supplied by the Royal Australian Navy, and a few of the ships were handed over to the Australian Government. Lloyds' Shipping List for 1920 showed 20 ex-German ships as belonging to the Commonwealth Line and, by 1924, this number had been reduced by six. In Lloyd's 1926 listings, only four of the ships remained. These were — *Booral, Boorara, Bulla* and *Carina*.

The huge volumes and supplements of Lloyd's shipping registers have always been carefully compiled. In the years 1920 to 1926 when large fleets of vessels were changing hands at a bewildering rate, Lloyds did their best. A period of months passed before the listings were received by Lloyds. They could only print the information they had. The year 1926 saw the Commonwealth Line reduced to seven ships — the five "Bays" and the two "Dales". From 1922 onwards the fleet had been reduced with such rapidity that Lloyds' Australian correspondents found it hard to keep abreast with the changing situation.

Komet, whilst not taking part in the cargo carrying activities of the Commonwealth Line, was a most interesting ship and served Australia continuously from 1914 to 1953. This twin screw ship was built in 1911 by Bremen-Vulcan, Vegesack. Her dimensions were 977 tons gross, 538 tons net, length 210 feet 3 inches, breadth 31 feet, depth 21 feet. *Komet* was the German Government Yacht stationed in New Guinea and was requisitioned by the Commonwealth Government when the German New Guinea Territories were annexed by Australia in 1914. *Komet* was re-named *Una* and served as a Government Supply Ship. Her name appeared on the fleet list of the Australian Commonwealth Line in 1916 and a few years later transferred to the Port Phillip Bay Pilot Service. Again her name was changed to one she retained for the remainder of her long and active life — *Akuna*. She served as senior pilot vessel at Port Phillip until the arrival in 1953 from Scotland of the new pilot vessel *Wyuna*. During the Second World War *Akuna* also took over as the Port examination ship under the white ensign. The name *Akuna* still lives on. It was given to the corvette *Gladstone* which was converted to act as relief pilot ship at Port Phillip to replace *Victoria* which finished 50 years service in the Victorian Pilot service in 1950.

Griefswald, built at Vegesack in 1907 and owned by Norddeutscher Lloyd, was quite a large ship, of 5,486 tons gross, 3,437 tons net. She was captured at Fremantle on 6 August 1914, taken over by the Navy and given the number C.10. This was later changed to the more lyrical name *Carina.* In 1915 *Carina* lost her naval identity, but remained around Europe as a cargo carrier. The ship struck a submerged object whilst voyaging from Cardiff to Port Said. After some repairs at Gibraltar, *Carina* resumed the voyage. She also had her share of crew trouble — a replacement crew took over at Durban. *Carina* returned to Australia to help move the wheat harvest to Europe and continued on the Australia-Europe general cargo run till 1924. *Carina* included the main Australian ports on her sailing schedules. She appeared to make much faster passages than the "Australs" and had more 'tween deck space, thus making loading and discharging easier at the various ports of call. *Carina* passed to Green ownership in 1924 to become *Captain Rokos.* Under this name, the vessel was wrecked near Monte Video on 17 February 1931. One of Brisbane's newer suburbs is named *Carina* but I doubt whether those responsible for the nomenclature did so in honour of s.s. *Carina* of the Australian Commonwealth Shipping Line.

s.s. *Cannstatt,* built in 1913, was a steamer of 5,930 tons gross, 3,699 tons net and owned by Norddeutscher Lloyd. Much of her cargo space was fitted for the carrying of frozen cargoes. In August, 1914 *Cannstatt* had reached the terminal port of Brisbane on her regular Hamburg-Australia voyage. At the outbreak of war, loading was stopped and the ship laid up at the A.U.S.N. Dolphins just off Brisbane's Botanic Gardens. Within a few weeks, the holds had been converted to troop decks and horse stalls and, in December, *Cannstatt* sailed for Egypt. She remained a troop ship until May, 1918, when the ship's name was changed to *Bakara* and placed under the flag of the Australian Commonwealth Line. Having so much refrigerated space *Bakara* was kept busy for several years. Gladstone in Queensland was a regular port of call. Her sailings to and from Australia were via Capetown and the cargoes of wool were unloaded at Hull. *Bakara* gave good service to the Commonwealth Line until sold to the Poland Line of Bremen in 1925. This Company changed the ship's name to *Witell* in 1936. s.s. *Witell* ex *Bakara,* ex *Cannstatt,* was sold to the Hamburg South American Line for their River Plate service. *Witell,* given the name *Rosario,* was in German waters when World War 2 started. *Rosario* was bombed and badly damaged in 1945, and lay at the Hamburg Docks for two years. Another change of owners, another change of name, and *Rosario* sailed under the flag of Finland as *Albertina.* At the age of forty-three, this staunch rover of the seven seas was bought by the Helsingfors Co. of Helsinki and a few months later as s.s. *Kotka,* sold to the British Ministry of Transport. The obituary of s.s. *Kotka,* ex s.s. *Albertina,* ex s.s. *Rosario,* ex s.s. *Witell,* ex s.s. *Bakara,* ex s.s. *Canstatt* —

> In July, 1956, loaded with chemicals and obsolete explosives, she made her last voyage to the South Atlantic and was scuttled in three miles depth of the ocean.   Rest after toil

s.s. *Tural,* built in 1907 by R. Craggs & Sons Ltd. of Middlesborough, was a ship of 3,530 tons gross. In August 1914 *Tural,* owned by the Austrian Lloyd Co. was requisitioned by the Commonwealth Government for use as a supply ship, later joining the Commonwealth Line's armada of wheat ships as *Carawa.* Returning from a wheat voyage to Europe, *Carawa* loaded a full cargo of 5,000 tons of case oil for Australia at New York. On 21 March, 1920 she grounded on a reef in the Galapagos Group in the Pacific. Rocks pierced the forehold which filled with water. A few days after stranding *Carawa* and her valuable case oil cargo had become a total loss. Her crew found a populated island and were eventually taken to Ecuador and then back to Australia.

Another early casualty was suffered by the Commonwealth Line with the torpedoing of the ex-German *Conargo* off the Irish coast on 31 March 1918. Four boats were launched, but ten of the crew were killed by the explosion. *Conargo*, built in 1902, sailed under the German flag as *Altona*. She was captured whilst en route to Australia in August 1914, having left Lisbon on July 8.

s.s. *Hessen*, built in 1905 at Flensburgh, was another of the large ships built for the long voyages to Australia and the German colonies in New Guinea. The gross tonnage was 5,099 tons. The ship was owned by W. Schuchmann of Bremerhaven. As the war clouds gathered over Europe, *Hessen* left her final loading port, Antwerp for Australia on 19 July 1914. She arrived in Sydney to find a change of ownership in a changing world. *Hessen* was formally requisitioned on 3 September 1914 as A-45 an Army transport for troops and horses. A cargo of concentrates was also loaded into the lower holds, and served as ballast. A-45 left Melbourne for Egypt on 2 February 1915, made a fast voyage to Suez, and later joined a convoy of troopships for the Gallipoli landing. She remained at anchor off the landing beaches for some weeks, serving as a water supply ship and animal hospital. *Hessen* anchored at Kephalos Harbour until July 1915, and was then returned to Australian control and re-named *Bulla*. Several trooping voyages followed before requisitioning by the British Admiralty as a fleet collier, running between South Wales and Genoa. *Bulla* joined the fleet of the Commonwealth Line in 1917 to take part in reducing Australia's wheat storage and feeding the starving populations of Europe. *Bulla* was placed on the London-Brisbane via ports general cargo service. She was a fairly fast ship; sailing from London on 3 October 1920, she passed Capetown on the 27th of that month, arriving at Fremantle on 15 November. On 27 December of that year, *Bulla* was loading flour and general cargo at Albany for discharge at Hull and London. She completed her loading at Fremantle early in the new year and arrived at London on 9 March to complete discharging of cargo, then commenced loading for Adelaide, Melbourne, Launceston, Hobart and Sydney. Further loadings were made at Newport, Liverpool, Glasgow and Newcastle-on-Tyne. *Bulla* apart from her capacious holds with a loaded draft of 26 feet 5 inches, also had large bunker space, enabling the ship to sail direct to Europe without any delays at Durban for refuelling with inferior coal. In 1924 *Bulla* returned to the fatherland and was renamed *Weissessee*, under the ownership of W. Schuchmann of Bremen, only a few miles from her birthplace Wesermunde. Under the German flag, the ship carried on her world voyaging. In 1943, whilst at Hamburg, the 38 year old ship was sunk during an air raid. Her battered hulk was raised in 1949, scrapped and fed into the blast furnaces of industrial Germany to make steel for the busy shipyards of Wesermunde.

s.s. *Melbourne* built in 1910, was another of the large modern German ships which happened to be in Australian water in August, 1914. *Melbourne*, a vessel of 5,926 tons gross and 3,710 tons net, was launched at Flensburgh, the main seaport of Schleswig-Holstein. The ship had been named after Victoria's capital city, having been designed for the Australian trade. After being requisitioned by the Australian Government it was decided *Melbourne* could no longer sail under that name as some confusion would result. *H.M.A.S. Melbourne,* an 8 inch gun cruiser, was on convoy escort in the Indian Ocean. The big German freighter became *Boonah* — thus a country town in Queensland with a population of just over 2,000 had the distinction of having the ex s.s. *Melbourne* named after it. *Boonah* became another of the "Black Germans", hauling troops, equipment, horses and fodder to the battlefields of the Middle East. This ship also had refrigerated holds and could supply an army with fresh food as an alternative to the bully beef and biscuits and other traditional military rations. When the German and Turkish armies collapsed and the Armistice was declared *Boonah* took over a part of a regular Australia-Europe wool and frozen produce service — her voyages from Melbourne to Dunkirk took less than two months.

The ex-German section of the Australian Commonwealth Line appeared to have been a profitable one. Their speed, types of cargo-spaces and loading gear put them in a class well above that of the "Australs". During the years of war and the submarine peril, they served the Allied cause well. Many factors were against the smooth running of the Commonwealth Line in the immediate post-war years. The world-wide and deadly influenza epidemic was the first of these. In the confines of the ships the disease decimated entire crews. On a coal burning ship there was no press button automation; brute strength, sweat and endurance sent the ships along. Each man had his part to play and sickness in a small percentage of the crew meant the working of double watches in the stokeholds and bunkers. Many men died on the job trying to raise enough steam to give the ships steerage way. Nothing in the scanty medicine chests of the ships could give relief, schedules were forgotten and survival of the ships and their crews was the paramount issue. *Boonah* had crew losses, but survived to face the mounting industrial unrest which dominated the post war waterfront scene in the ports of Australia. The Stewards and Pantrymen's Union put in a log of claims early in 1919. The coastal shipping companies agreed to their demands, the Commonwealth Line refused, but after a few days, they also acceded. The example of the Stewards and Pantrymen's Union was followed by the Seamen's Union with similar results. Still the ships did not sail, — the Merchant Officers Guild stated their claims, followed by the Marine Engineers. In this series of strikes the Commonwealth ships were held up for six weeks. All the planned schedules were abandoned, as the cargoes had been taken by ships of other nations.

Yet another feature of those post war years were the numerous fires which flared up in the bunkers of the ex-German ships, whether some expatriate from the fatherland resented his country's ships sailing under the Australian flag, or the crews wanting more time in port is not known. The fires usually occurred while the ships were in Sydney. After extinguishing a difficult blaze in the bunkers of s.s. *Boonah,* advertisements were placed in the newspapers of Sydney by the Commonwealth Government offering a reward of £100 for information leading to the apprehension of the culprit. Poor ventilation in the bunkers could have been the cause, or the loading of fresh stocks of coal on top of fuel which had been on the ship for months.

With all these vicissitudes plus the usual perils of the sea, *Boonah* continued as a profitable venture until the affairs of the line were placed in the hands of the Board of Directors under the Commonwealth Shipping Act of 1923. Rationalisation followed, and *Boonah* was taken over by Norddeutscher Lloyd, to continue trading on the Trans-Atlantic route as *Witram.*

s.s. *Bulga* was the only German ship to retain her original name whilst in the service of the Commonwealth Line. She was a small ship of 1,449 tons gross and 907 tons net, with a length of just over 250 feet. Built in 1903 by Howaldstkerke of Kiel, her crew accommodation seems to have been sub-standard. While in Australian waters her sailing dates were often posponed by crew trouble — this could mean anything from the cook's hangover to a full scale mutiny. *Bulga* also had some passenger accommodation and served on the Sydney-Ocean Island phosphate route. Occasionally *Bulga* sailed on the Gilbert Islands trade until 1923. I have been unable to find out where this 20-year wanderer of the seas went to when the Commonwealth Line disposed of her. It seems that the passing of this prosaic freighter did not merit a line of newsprint.

s.s. *Prinz Zigmund*, a twin screw steamer of 3,302 tons gross, was built in 1903. She served for a while on the general cargo service to Europe, was then sold to the Western Australian Government for their coastal service and sailed under the name of *Bambra*. The peculiarities of the West Australian Coastal trade required a particular type of ship. The ability to stay afloat in the worst possible seas was the first consideration. To be small enough to use the north-west ports was second, to carry both cargo and passengers and to have shelter decks to house several hundred head of cattle. Last, but not least, the ship had to be able to stay alongside the wharf sitting on the harbour floor without straining the hull, as tides recede for some miles leaving ships high and dry. That part of the Australian coast is noted for its cyclones which build up with speed and ferocity. The cyclone of 1910 was responsible for the loss of s.s. *Koombana* a new ship of 3,668 tons, and the entire complement of 120 passengers and crew. *Koombana* had left Port Hedland for Broome and was never sighted again. The A.U.S.N. Cargo ship *Moira* was also in the region at the time but managed to make port with her funnel blown over the side and her cargo of cattle dead or maimed from the buffeting. *Bambra* served the West Australian Government well until relieved by the newly built *Koolinda* of 4,227 tons in 1926. *Bambra* sailed to Singapore, then to parts unkown.

Another of the small German ships was *Germania* 1,096 tons gross, 538 tons net. Whilst in the Commonwealth fleet as *Mawatta* she served on the Australian Coast until superseded by the D class ships. She was then chartered to J.P. Boyd for a year or so, and finally sold to James Patrick & Co. for their Melbourne to Brisbane cargo service.

s.s. *Wildenfels,* built in 1901 by Swan Wigham of Newcastle-on-Tyne for German buyers, a large vessel of 5,512 tons gross 3,586 net, was yet another valuable acquisition by the Commonwealth Line for their European service as s.s. *Gilgai.* Like the other ships on that service, it was found to be more economical to use the Cape route in preference to the Suez. No doubt the toilers in the stokeholds and bunkers also preferred the longer but cooler way to and from Australia. *Gilgai* was not a fast ship — 19 days from Capetown to Fremantle was fair steaming — but of longer duration than that of the mail ships. The ex-German ships had to visit numerous ports around Europe to complete their loadings, but usually sailed with packed holds. During 1923 and 1924 modern new ships to replace the war-time losses were being completed in ever increasing number, all oil burners, requiring small crews. *Gilgai,* of 1901 vintage, was outclassed for the regular general cargo service and transferred back to German ownership.

s.s. *Pfalz*, requisitioned at Melbourne within minutes of the declaration of war on 4 August 1914, was without doubt a prize ship in every way. Launched in 1913 at the yards of Bremer-Vulcan, Vesesack, with a tonnage of 6,750 gross and 4,083 net, with refrigerated holds, *Pfalz* could be described as the finest of her type in the world. Had she been allowed to leave Port Phillip that day, *Pfalz* would have made an ideal store ship for Von Spee's squadron which was in the Pacific at that time. Full use of the ship was made by the Australian Defence Forces, as the 16 German ships were responsible for the rapid despatch of supplies to the A.I.F. in the Middle East. Apart from their war winning efforts, they gave the Commonwealth Line five years of excellent service during the post-war shipping boom. *Pfalz* sailed under the name of *Boorara* as part of the 79,792 gross tons of ex-German shipping which formed such a vital part of the Commonwealth Line. Their deadweight capacity was 124,487 tons with 390,016 cubic feet of refrigerated space.

The financial statement of 30 June 1923 shows profit on ex-enemy vessels at £3,673,494. This amount represented a huge sum in the year 1923 when £3 was considered a good week's wages. Yet the Australian Commonnwealth Line is recorded in history as a failure. The Line did not die a natural death; it was assassinated.

Boorara was the only Australian ship to make Mauritius a port of call for discharge of frozen produce. Avonmouth appears to have been her chief port of discharge in Britain, and calls were also made at Liverpool and Glasgow. With the completion of *Ferndale* and *Fordsdale,* ships which specialised in frozen cargoes, *Boorara* was sold to Em-Hadjllias, her name changed to *Nereus* and her port of registry became Syra.

s.s. *Berlin* of 1904 was a medium sized cargo ship of 4,229 tons gross and 2,605 net Not a pretentious vessel to be named after Germany's capital city, she was built at Flensburgh. *Berlin* was an early requisition and was given the name *Parattah* After the years of war service, the ship arrived at Newcastle-on-Tyne on 17 January 1921 with the usual load of wheat. Three months were spent on the Tyne installing new furnaces. Her name does not appear on subsequent sailing lists and, like the "Australs", cargo from Europe was hard to find for this type of ship, so *Parattah* of Sydney was sold in 1922.

Another Flensburgh built ship, *Neuminster* of 4,224 tons gross and 2,635 tons net, launched in 1907, was requisitioned in Sydney on 4 August 1918. She took over the typical Australian name *Cooee,* the only one so named according to Lloyds' Shipping register. She was just another solid looking German tramp steamer, reliable if not rapid. In between European wool and wheat voyages *Cooee* put in some time hauling coal and concentrates around the southern coast of Australia. Early in 1921 she spent some months in Britain having new furnaces installed. In the seven years of service to Australia, many thousands of tons of coal had been shovelled into those furnaces, each of the fires cleaned out every four hours, ashes wetted down and hoisted into the world's oceans. The boilers are the heart of a ship and old age usually takes its toll there. A condition something like hardening of the arteries also takes place in the condenser tubes. They can be patched up or replaced, but it becomes a continuing process. Every ship of the Commonwealth Line had to undergo a periodic survey by Lloyds, the surveys becoming more frequent as age increased. Mediterranean and Chinese owners did not insure their ships, and so were free to sail them until the boilers collapsed or blew up. So for many years Australian owners have fulfilled Lloyds' fullest requirements and when this was no longer economically feasible, sold their ships overseas at scrap prices. *Cooee* sailed away from Australia into this jungle of foreign shipping, taking her Australian name with her. Ships are no longer given such picturesque names. The Cunard Line have given their latest cruise ship the name *Cunard Adventurer* following the modern trend of including the owner's name in that of the ship.

The remaining German ships of the Commonwealth Line performed similar voyages as those already described. They came, they worked, they went, in the all too short history of the Line.

Toromeo, a 1905 product of the Tyneside firm of Wigham, Richardson & Co., was sailing under the German flag with the proud name of *Tiberius*. She was a late comer to the fleet of the Commonwealth Line. Being a part of the reparation deal of 1919, *Araluen* of 1901, a large cargo vessel of 5,519 tons gross, roamed the seas when the maps showed the North Sea as the German Ocean, her name was then *"Scharzfels"*. *"Barambah"* was another of the valuable refrigeration ships; her tonnage of 5,928 tons gross secured the ship a place in the troop convoys. Under German ownership, she had sailed under the name of *Hobart*.

s.s. *Oberhausen,* of 1905, a Tyne built ship of 4,322 tons gross was loading apples at Port Huon, Tasmania when war was declared. Requisitioned by the Navy and given a number and a coat of grey paint, she sailed as a troop and horse transport. The Australian Light Horse Regiments were over in the Middle East by Christmas, 1914. Thousands of horses were required and the ex-German ships were most suitable for such requirements. Numbers created some confusion and eventually *Oberhausen* took the name *Booral*. After some months of idleness in Sydney Harbour, the ship was sold to Greek buyers in 1924. *Booral* became *Atlas* of the Port of Syra, under the ownership of Em-Hadjillas, who had also bought *Boorara. Sumatra* of 1913 arrived at Sydney on 30 July 1914, the largest of the German ships, her tonnage being 7,484 gross and 4,672 net. As *Barungra,* she was placed under the management of the Australian Government and made a few war-time voyages. However, *Barungra* was never in the fleet of the Commonwealth Line and may have become a war casualty before its formation. *Moora,* ex-*Lothringen,* built in 1906 at Bremen, and *Dongarra,* built at Flensburgh in 1906 as *Stolzenfels* were almost identical and served the Commonwealth Line until 1924.

Osnabruck was also in the peaceful harbour of Sydney in August 1914. This ship, yet another product of the Flensburgh shipyards, was built in 1907, a medium sized cargo ship of 4,240 gross and 2,369 net tonnage. Re-named *Calulu* she played her part as one of the wool and wheat armada. In the pre-synthetic days wool was of paramount importance in the equipment of the armed forces. On the western front sheepskin coats were issued to the troops during the bitter winter campaigns. These were part of the cargoes of the ships of the Commonwealth. Profits of war time and the post-war period disappeared in the early twenties. Many of the crews of the Australian ships had served years on ships under British Board of Trade conditions known as "pound and pint", due to the prescribed ration scale. Lime juice was issued a few days out from port as fresh provisions were replaced by salted meats and other preserved foods. In U.S.A. British ships were usually referred to as "Limejuicers", now abbreviated to

"Limeys". Scurvy, a disease once common amongst seamen and caused by vitamin deficiencies, was prevented by liberal issues of lime juice.

One cannot write the history of the ships of the Commonwealth Line without giving some of the story of the men who manned them. They have been blamed for the Line's demise and I would like to write a few words for the defence.

Waterfront work, including that of seamen, has always been on a casual basis. This has meant the perpetuation of the attitudes that are inseparable from the "casual" system and has resulted in the Seamen's and other waterside unions becoming isolated from the rest of industry. They have been described as a highly volatile body of men, impatient of regulation, distrustful of any authority, and fearful of change. It is true that the maritime unions work in the closest unity for mutual defence and support. The waterfront society has been known for many years as a world narrow in horizons, but rich in character. Since the early days of William Morris Hughes, the maritime unions of Australia have been well organised. By virtue of this, they have been able to secure good working conditions and maintain them. The Commonwealth Navigation Act gave the Australian coastal shipping companies the complete monopoly of both the passenger and cargo trade around the coast of Australia. Having this, the companies were able to build well found fleets of ships, and man them under conditions which were a vast improvement on those which were tolerated by the crews of overseas shipping lines. The ships of the Commonwealth Line operating on overseas routes were at a disadvantage. No subsidies were paid by the Federal Government. Management did try to economise, but the crews on the Australian ships saw these economies as a lowering of standards to those they had endured for years with the overseas companies. They always had the complete support of the Waterside Workers' Federation, so that any attempt to have crews signed on overseas under British Board of Trade conditions would have resulted in a complete black ban. The Australian maritime unions had fought for many years to get what they enjoyed and looked upon any scaling down as a betrayal of those who had led them in the big strikes of the 1880's. On the coal burning ships men were worn out before they reached the age of 50. The same applied to the seamen — they were not chipping and painting all the time; much of their work was in preparing the ship for cargo, removing and replacing hatch boards and beams, and rigging derricks — all jobs which required strength and agility; attributes which decrease with age. The second engineer selected the stokehold crew and the first mate was responsible for the deckhands. As both of these officers had the responsibility of getting the maximum effort out of the crew, and promotions to Chief Engineer and Captain depended on their performance, they favoured the younger and more active applicants. As the entire crew were signed off on the completion of each voyage, this gave the opportunity to drop the crew members unable to cope with the arduous toil. Unlike the maritime unions of Australia, the British unions lacked both funds and solidarity and, as long as shipowners kept within the spartan limits of the Board of Trade Agreement, nothing could be done by the unions. Certain shipping companies had very bad reputations — "no names, no court martial". A very small minority were excellent employers — jobs were hard to obtain on their ships — they manned on the father and son tradition. Bonuses were paid for special cargoes, food was always fresh and plentiful, and during the time in their home port, crews were kept in employment at short pay rates instead of being unemployed for that period. The following two chapters are factual to the seafaring conditions of the 1920's when the Commonwealth Line's trade graph was showing a rapid decline; and may serve to illustrate why the crews of the Australian ships showed a lack of enthusiasm for any rationalisation programme.

Chapter 5

COAL BURNING SHIPS

The attendance of applicants for crew vacancies at the offices of the Mercantile Marine in seaports only started during the Second World War, when labour, along with all other commodities, was impressed. Previous to this, the seaman studied shipping lists in the free library, and trudged around the miles of docks looking for his job. In the case of a seaman, he would approach the Chief Officer of the ship; firemen, trimmers and greasers would see the Second Engineer. Should there be any vacancies, and their Discharge Books satisfactory, the prospective crew would be told when and where the ship would be signing on. The National Sailors & Firemen's Union did not assist in this regard; their representative was very much in evidence at the "Pay Off" on completion of the voyage when Union Dues were collected. Having signed on and passed the Doctor — the latter ritual took approximately 30 seconds per crew member, three words being spoken by the Doctor, "Cough, "Again" and "Next", — aboard ship, firemen, trimmers and greasers were assembled on the after deck. The three watch-keeping Engineers, 2nd, 3rd and 4th were in attendance. The Second Engineer had the advantage of knowledge gained from Discharge Books sighted on engagement, and further advantage of first choice from the assembly. Stokehold and engine room crew worked four hours on and eight hours off. The Second's watch was the four to eight, he selected his four firemen, two trimmers and one greaser. The Third's watch was twelve to four, he took his crew. The Fourth's watch was eight to twelve and consisted of the remnants.

To the uninitiated the work in a stokehold appears to be for unskilled labour; this is far from being the case. The poise, stance, and the correct flick of the wrists as the coal left the shovel to be correctly spread over the entire surface of the furnace grate was all important to good firing, which in brief was the art of getting the maximum steam from the minimum amount of coal. A ship at sea is not a stable platform on which to perform acrobatics and to see a good fireman in action in the bowels of a coal burning ship, as he times and anticipates the movement of the ship, was truly seeing the "Dignity of Labour". The fireman does not move from the front of the boilers, except for copious draughts of oatmeal and water, and a few minutes standing under a ventilator. Coal is brought to him by the trimmer from the bunkers, a distance of anything up to 50 yards. Bunkers are illuminated by the trimmer's "Slush Lamp", a device which consists of a can of old waste oil with a thick wick protruding therefrom. As the ship pitches and rolls across the miles of ocean, he is down there with his barrow, shovel, his thoughts and his slush lamp surveying the two thousand tons of coal which, with his help, will pass through the ship's furnaces during the next four weeks. The rattling of a shovel on the steel plates of the stokehold brings him back to reality. It is the traditional signal of the fireman and means more coal. Half an hour before the end of each watch the scene in the stokehold represents Dante's Inferno. Fires are cleaned, ashes drawn from beneath the grates, and wetted down with sea water. The air is sulphurous and thick with fine ash which passes up through the ventilators to the boat deck, giving annoyance to passengers playing deck quoits. The deck of the stokehold is covered with wet ashes, the consistency of hot porridge. This is shovelled into bags and hoisted up to the main deck and dumped into the sea. At the end of the four hour watch, firemen and trimmers retreat to their quarters over the stern of the ship. "Showers" in the coal burning days were the exception rather than the rule. Each man drew a bucket of water from the tap in the alleyway outside the galley door. The ablutions were a small section of the forecastle, with a board along one side recessed to hold the buckets. A steam pipe was used to heat the water. A quick all over wash with a sweat rag and the remaining water tipped over the head completed the toilet. Soap was not supplied, the crew supplied their own. Stockhold crews were easily recognised even in shore going rig; a dehydrated look and ingrained coal dust defied any toiletry aids. During the Second Engineer's watch 4 to 8, the ship made her best speed, as invariably this watch consisted of well experienced and muscular firemen and trimmers. The Fourth's watch, 8 to 12, consisted of beginners, and men well past their prime for such arduous work. On the Atlantic Flyer's such as *Mauretania, Lusitania,* etc., each of which consumed 480 tons of coal for every day of steaming, Junior Engineers were in charge of each boiler room, their job being to regulate the stoking and cleaning of fires. They kept time with a gong, the firemen worked in unison to its beat; the more steam required the faster the tempo. Similar stimulation was used on the galleys of Ancient Rome, a drum being used to regulate the required stroke of the oarsmen. Further encouragement was given by the "Master" who walked along the platform between the rowers wielding his whip.

Returning to the stokeholds of ships of 1930 the "Four to Eight" was always referred to as the "Black Pan Watch". Their job was to keep the galley bunkers filled. Crew food was always spartan; most commodities supplied to the ship were distinctly labelled "Crew" or "Cabin" and showed a great variation in quality. Many cargo ships on regular routes also carried 12 passengers at First Class Rates, consequently meals served in the Saloon and Engineers' Mess Rooms were varied, well cooked and offered at least three choices for each course. This inevitably meant a fair quantity of each meal was not used. Cooks and stewards partook of some of this — the remainder was stacked into a black baking dish on the galley shelf. Each evening at eight, this was collected by the 4 to 8 watch of firemen and trimmers and became their supper in lieu of the "Scouse" or "Dry Hash" with which the remainder of the crew had regaled themselves two hours before. This "Crumbs from the Rich Man's Table" may not sound compatible with the picture I have portrayed of the Dignity of Labour, as the stokers do their vital share of toil in getting the ship from point A to point B along the sea routes of the world. A Liverpool — Irish stoker was anything but servile. He worked hard, drank hard, and took a fierce delight in his prowess; and to achieve a place in the "Black Pan Watch" was a distinction. Apart from the "Saloon Dinner" each night, which was all wholesome and unspoilt food, they also had 7 hours of unbroken sleep during the night while at sea, or 7 hours sampling the nocturnal delights of the ship's ports of call. The Second Engineer, confident of the abilities of his selected crew, seldom left the Engine Room to visit the stokehold during his watch. Deck Officers, proud of their snowy white decks and gleaming paintwork, complained bitterly about trimmers emerging from the depths of the ship to the height of the boat deck to trim ventilators on to the wind, and thus make conditions below a little more tenable, leaving a trail of black boot marks across a freshly holystoned deck, and grimy hand prints on newly painted ventilators. Another source of annoyance was the hanging of stokehold clothing over the white rails around the stern. To all complaints the "Second" would reply with a bland smile, and a promise to do something about it. Like the Captain, the "Chief Engineer" was a remote figure, only seen down below in emergencies. He did not frequent the Engineers' Mess Room, but dined in the saloon with the Captain and Deck Officers. He had no watchkeeping duties but his vast knowledge, acquired over many years of hard won experience, was there if necessary. He spent the days in his cabin working on problems of fuel consumption, defect lists and reading detective novels.

Through the windows of the shipping office the murky winter sky of the Liverpool waterfront did little to lighten the room designed for the "signing on" routine of those "who go down to the sea in ships". A gusty wind blew a mixture of sleet, soot and rain against the window panes. Inside, the fumes of a kerosene heater combined with the smoke from plug tobacco, and a smell of stale beer. The occasion was the signing on of the crew of s.s. *Matina* 2,620 tons net, Port of Registry, Newcastle, voyage 190, to Santa Marta, a banana port on the Atlantic Coast of Colombia. Behind the desk stood the Shipping Master reading out the various clauses of the Board of Trade Agreement; it was just a ritual performed several times a day, they had to be read, but the garbled monotone was audible only to those within a few feet of him. Not that it mattered, the crew knew it all by heart, every six weeks through the year, just a part of their nomadic existence. The firemen and sailors mutually agreed to assist each other. The firemen shall keep the galley supplied with coal etc. etc. The crew of 44 stood around their various groups, by choice and custom, not by regulation. Firemen, trimmers, greasers and donkeymen on one side of the room, bosun, carpenter and seamen on the other. In one corner a group of deck officers, in the other the engineers. At the far end, stewards, cooks and engineers' messman looked somewhat isolated. The two wireless operators, both "First Trippers" appeared both despondent and apprehensive as they surveyed the various groups, men with whom they had to live for the next 5 weeks. The Captain, referred to in the agreement as "The Master" and on the Bills of Lading as "Master Under God", was behind the desk with the Shipping Master. In a few minutes each of the 44 crew members would have signed on to "Obey all his lawful commands". At present, he was gazing at the clock wondering if he would be able to catch the 12 o'clock train to Southport. The last of the 48 clauses was read. Officers and engineers moved forward to sign followed by the rest of the crew, the last to sign being the deck boy. Each man was given an "Advance Note" of half a month's pay as he surrendered his Discharge Book.

At that period, 1928, A.B.'s and firemen were paid £8.10s.0d — per month, Trimmers 10s.0d. less. The Deck Boy once again was at the bottom of the list with £3.10s.0d per month. The advance notes were in the form of a cheque cashable 3 days after s.s. *Matina* had left the River Mersey. The discharge books were placed in the charge of the 2nd mate for the voyage, who made the necessary notations and returned them to the crew at the pay off at the final port of discharge. Thus, if any members of the crew failed to join, the advance note was not paid, his Discharge Book, his only means of livelihood, could only be claimed when the ship returned, marked "Failed to Join", equivalent to a D-R or a Black Discharge. The Advance Notes were inteded to be cashed by Wives and Sweethearts, but out side the door of the shipping office that well known Mersey side character "Jaffe" was waiting to cash them at a discount of 2/- in the £. An interest of 10% for 4 days provided him with a comfortable living. In 1928, with the post war shipping boom a thing of the past, every estuary and backwater around the British Isles had its rows of laid up ships. Jobs were hard to get and not lightly cast aside so that Jaffe and his ilk took an almost negligible risk. The crew were to join at one minute past midnight on the following morning. The articles just signed clearly stated "No overtime shall be paid on day of sailing or Day of arrival". Seamen instead of working their normal 12 hour day would work for the full 24 hours. At midnight *Matina* was under the "Tips" having just completed loading 2,000 tons of bunker coal, her white superstructure looked a sorry sight, her decks a litter of wires, coal, hatch boards and beams. The "Shore Crowd" had finished with her, *Matina* was ready for her crew. They came aboard, a motley crew, mostly muffled against the elements, cloth cap, muffler, and Military Overcoat, which were then selling at 4/6 each. The war to end war had finished 10 years before. The seamen lived forward under the raised forecastle, the firemen and trimmers aft in a deckhouse over the stern. *Matina* had been built in 1904, when sailing ships still carried much of the world's commerce. Sailors were still resentful of the change from sail to steam, and with reluctance signed on the steamers. It was many years before oil and water mixed and in the interests of harmony owners designed their ships to give the maximum distance between sailors and stokers. Hence the clause "Firemen and Sailors mutually agree to assist each other". They never did, but the Master could use it to maintain peace between the two factions. Bedding issue was a simple proceeding; — a strong coarse mattress cover and pillow case of the same material, and two grey army blankets. As each man drew his bedding issue from the steward he passed on to the fore deck. There he helped himself, from a huge bale, to as much straw as the mattress and pillow would hold. In the fo'csle the top bunks were annexed by the senior A.B's; once again the deck boy had his choice, Hobson's Choice, the last bunk, a lower one positioned in such a way that the contents of the mess table usually landed in it as *Matina* rolled her way across the Western Ocean. Half an hour after midnight, the Bosun appeared in the alleyway with a laconic "Say Fellers, lets go". The hours went by, gradually order came out of chaos, and *Matina* began to look more like a ship than a junk yard. By 9 p.m. she was in all respects ready for sea. Tugs alongside and the lock gates open as the evening tide reached full flood. The clock in the Royal Liver Building showed 10, as *Matina* **steamed down the Mersey, the trams at the pier head and the bright lights of Liverpool looking colourful through the rain. Distance does lend enchantment to the view. Derricks had been double lashed, all moveable gear stowed away and a force 9 gale was blowing. In the fo'csle port holes and deadlights had been screwed up with Marlin spikes. Ventilators were unshipped and painted canvas lashed around the openings. The smell of oilskins, pipe tobacco, sweat and cabbage competed with that of sulphur. The living spaces of the ship had been** fumigated with sulphur candles; it made no difference, the bugs always survived and came out fighting. *Matina* curtseyed as she breasted the swell of the channel passed the lightships and into Liverpool Bay, where the pilot cutter on station off the Coast of Anglesey lay waiting to take off *Matina's* Pilot, her last link with the shore. The ponderous beat of her triple expansion reciprocating engine soon reached its maximum of 72 Revs per minute, which pushed the vessel through the ocean at a speed of 10 knots into the turbulence of the Irish Sea. *Matina* had commenced voyage 190.

Chapter 6

SAILING SHIPS AND VESSELS

The original programme for shipbuilding in Australia was for 48 vessels, 24 were to be steel cargo steamers, and 24 wooden sailing vessels with auxiliary power. The post war shipping slump came with such rapidity that the contracts for building 22 of the wooden sailing ships were cancelled. The two ships already nearing completion at the yards of Messrs Kidman & Mayoh of Sydney, were five masted schooners. These ships had a deadweight capacity of 2,600 tons. Other dimensions were length 232 feet, breadth 42 feet 8 inches. The auxiliary power was to be supplied by two sets of 250 H.P. engines of semi-diesel pattern, giving the vessels a speed of 7 knots when under power. Four ship building firms had been awarded a contract to each build six of these ships. They were as follows:-

Hughes, Martin & Washington Ltd. of Sydney.
W.A. Shipbuilding Co. of Fremantle.
Wallace Power Boat Co. of Sydney.
Kidman & Mayoh of Sydney.

The vessels were to be built of Australian hardwood.

The two ships launched at the yards of Messrs Kidman & Mayoh on the Parramatta River were to have been barquentines. In the interests of economy they were rigged as schooners. As a further concession to the shortage of finance, it was decided to dispense with the auxiliary power. They were launched as *Braeside* and *Burnside* the only offspring of a grandiose scheme. It was obvious that sail could no longer compete, and doubtless the decision to cancel the contracts was the right one.

Braeside and *Burnside* played little part in the history of the Commonwealth Line; they remained in the fleet for a few months and their subsequent movements are shrouded in mystery. I believe they served along the Pacific Coast of North America; they would have been too large for the Pacific Island trade.

John Murray. Built at Glasgow as *Loch Ryan*. Acquired by the Victorian Government in the pre-federation era for use as a boys' training ship. Purchased by Commonwealth Line July, 1917. Completely re-rigged for Trans-Pacific route. Wrecked on reef off Malden Island, 22 May 1918 whilst *en route* San Francisco to Melbourne with a cargo of engines and case oil. After an explosion in the cargo the vessel became a total loss. Ship's master Captain Vaughan, with two volunteers, made an open boat voyage of 500 miles to Fanning Island Cable Station. Another boat piloted by the Chief Mate reached Raratonga, Cook

Islands, and was picked up by s.s. *Moana.* Shipping authorities diverted s.s. *Macedon* to Malden Island to pick up the survivors from the *John Murray.* This was accomplished on 6 August 1918.

Louis Thierault. 440 tons. Built by A. Thierault, Nova Scotia, 1918. Owned by Hankinson Shipping Co. Ltd., Digby, Nova Scotia. Sold to Australian Government 1921. Sold to Capt. A.F. Watchlin of Auckland, 1922, for Australia-New Zealand Timber trade. Sold to Brisbane Timbers Ltd. 1926.

Cardinia. 1915 tons, ex-German ship *Olinda.* Steel construction built 1903 by A. Rodger & Co., Glasgow. Registered under Commonwealth ownership at Port of Sydney. This ship was acquired by the Australian Government in 1917. Considerable difficulty was experienced in obtaining skilled crews for the sailing ships and *Olinda,* along with other wind powered units of the fleet, was disposed of very early in the history of the Commonwealth Line.

Speedway. Another blue nose schooner, built of wood in 1917 in Nova Scotia, previously owned by S. St C. Jones, Little Brook, Nova Scotia. She was a three masted vessel of 622 tons gross, length 155 feet, breadth 33 feet 3 inches, depth 17 feet 2 inches. In the brief period *Speedway* was owned by the Commonwealth Line, she was registered in Melbourne.

Shandon. This iron built three masted barque was launched at Glasgow in January, 1883, the builders being R. Duncan & Co. of Port Glasgow. Dimensions were 1470 tons gross, length 245 feet 9 inches, breadth 37 feet 8 inches, depth 21 feet 3 inches. *Shandon* had a long and hard working life. She made no record passages but survived all the hazards of the world's oceans and delivered her cargoes safely. At one period, she sailed under the name of *Victor*, but reverted to *Shandon* before joining the fleet of the Commonwealth Line in 1917, when her port of registry became Melbourne. In her trans-Pacific voyages she seems to have followed the same tracks and carried similar cargoes that sailing ships had done for the previous five decades. As an example, her voyage of 1920-21 can be given in some detail. After discharging coal from Newcastle, N.S.W., *Shandon* loaded nitrates at Iquique, Chile. Fully loaded, she sailed for San Francisco on 2 December 1920, discharged her cargo and took on ballast for a voyage to Eureka, California, arriving there on 26 December 1920. A full cargo of timber for Melbourne was then loaded. *Shandon* sailed from Eureka on 27 January 1921, arriving in Melbourne on 31 March. The list of movements of vessels some weeks later showed *Shandon* as still at her berth in the Yarra. "Future business not yet fixed." *Shandon* had made her last voyage under sail. She served as a coal hulk in various ports. At the outbreak of World War 2, she was moored at Port Adelaide. As the War spread into the Pacific, Townsville became one of the main ports for Australian troopships. A number of these were ex-coastal liners and were coal burners. Townsville lacked facilities for replenishing bunkers. *Shandon* was towed north from Adelaide to become a coaling station at the eastern end of the main Townsville wharf. Laying there, stripped of her topmasts, she was still a graceful ship, the poop deck and the somewhat ornate skylight showing something of her former glory. It is hard to summarise the part the sailing ships played in the Commonwealth Line. The balance sheets do not itemise individual ships earnings, apart from *Braeside* and *Burnside.* They were not costly ships and, used as a war time expedient, did their job.

24. T.S.S. *Indarra*, as Kobe-Keelung Liner s.s. *Horai Maru,* O.S.K. Line Official tonnage 9375: 451.0 x 60.1 x 37.4 feet. Engines quadruple expansion, twin sc; cylinders 26.5, 38, 59 and 76" x 48" stroke. Boilers, 7 single ended, 210 lb. She was beautifully fitted up and comfortable at sea, but was heavy on coal.

25. s.s. *Loongana*. Bass Straits Passenger and Cargo ship. On one occasion saved by Melbourne tugs when her coal supplies were exhausted.

26. The scuttling off Sydney Heads of the battle-cruiser *Australia* in 1924. The Australian fleet is saluting.

27. H.M.A.S. *Sydney*, which sailed with H.M.A.S. *Melbourne* with the first Australian convoy to the Middle East in 1914. Destroyed German cruiser *Emden* 9 November 1914.

28. s.s. *Sophocles*, 11,200 tons gross. Aberdeen Line. Built in 1922 by Harland and Wolff at Belfast. She was taken over by the Shaw Savill Company in 1926 and joined the fleet of the Aberdeen and Commonwealth Line and sailed with the five "Bays" and two "Dales" from 1928 onward.

29. s.s. *Matina*. 1910.

30. s.s. *Kanowna*. Melbourne–Cairns Passenger and Mail run, 1903-1929.

31. s.s. *Taroona*.

"WARATAH" – LUNDS BLUE ANCHOR LINE

This Company's ships were named after Australian towns, and designed and registered as emigrant carriers from London to Australia. On her maiden voyage on 5th November, 1908, in addition to her normal passenger complement, had 689 emigrants in dormitory accommodation in the holds. This was usual with the passenger-cargo ships of the time. This hold space was filled with cargo on the homeward voyage.

Waratah like her sister ship *Geelong* was of 6,004 tons net, her gross tonnage was 9,339.07 tons, with a speed of 13 knots.

Waratah after loading 6,500 tons of cargo at various Australian ports called into Durban on her return voyage to London. After bunkering, *Waratah* left Durban 8.15 p.m. on the 26th July, 1909 for Cape Town. On this short voyage she vanished. No wreckage was ever found and *Waratah* became another mystery of the sea. After this loss The Blue Anchor Line went out of the Australian Migrant Trade. The five remaining vessels were taken over by the P & O Company, and became known as the P & O Branch Line, maintaining the migrant service around the Cape from London to Brisbane. After World War 1, these vessels were replaced by one Class 13,000 ton ships, *Borda, Bendigo, Belfara, Barrabool* catering for the Australian migrant trade. In the depression years of the early 1930s, the Commonwealth Government cancelled assisted migration. The P & O Branch Line closed down, its ships were sold for scrap.

33   P & O SHIP AUSTRALIA (1)

1870. Was many years on UK-Australia Service, mainly from 1884. Wrecked Tasmania-1899.

"THEMISTOCLES"

11,250 tons. Aberdeen Line sister ship to *Demonsthenes*. Both ships commenced service about 1909. The Aberdeen Line was very early in the field of Migration to Australia. Two of their most famous sailing ships *Brilliant* and *Pericles* made swift passages with migrants, in the 1870s. In 1877 *Brilliant* made the passage from London to Sydney in 84 days.

The steamers of the Aberdeen Line commenced their voyages from Liverpool, calling at Teneriffe and Cape Town making Albany their first Australian port of call, Brisbane being their terminal port. In addition to a normal 300 third class and 100 first class, temporary accommodation was erected on the upper tween decks of Nos. 1 and 2 Holds. On the return voyage to Liverpool this was dismantled and the space used for wool cargoes. "*Euripedes*", 15,000 ton version of "Demosthenes" and "Themistocles" launched in 1914 was added to the fleet, and after war service as troopers, these three ships brought scores of thousands of migrants to all parts of Australia. "Themistocles", the last of the Aberdeen Line, made her last voyage in 1950. Funnel Colours "White Star" early 1930.

"QUETTA"

35   3,222 tons, one of the small fleet of ships designed to give Queensland a direct link with the U.K. Sponsored by the Queensland Government in the 1880s to bring migrants to Queensland ports. These ships sailed from London via Suez and Torres Strait, making Brisbane their terminal port. Known as the Queensland Steamship Line, they were a subsidiary of the British India Line and A.U.S.N. Co. *Quetta* was built by Denny Bros. of Dumbarton in 1881. After leaving Cooktown en route to London, *Quetta* struck an uncharted rock near Thursday Island and sank with a loss of 123 lives. This was on 18th February, 1890. Present day charts show the submerged rock as "Quetta" rock. A memorial also exists at the Anglican Church, Thursday Island to the victims of this disaster.

Chapter 7

THE AMERICAN PURCHASE, WOODEN MOTOR VESSELS AND STEAMERS

A contract was arranged between the Australian Government and the Sloan Shipyard Corporation of Seattle for the building of four wooden full powered motor vessels in November 1917. At this period of the war, losses of merchant ships through enemy action were catastrophic; this was the result of Germany's declaration of unrestricted submarine warfare. In one month, April, 1917, over one million tons of allied and neutral shipping was destroyed, causing the British Prime Minister to admit that if losses continued at this rate, Britain would be forced to ask Germany for a negotiated peace. At the height of this desperate situation Australia was looking for more ships. The American wooden ships were the only answer. These standardised vessels were of the following dimensions: 2368 tons (gross), 1820 tons (net), length 262 ft. 2 inches, breadth 46 feet 4 inches, depth 21 feet. Propulsion was by twin screw engines aft in the steamships. Power was generated in two water tube boilers. The four ships from Sloan's were delivered as follows: *Cethana*, 18 July 1918; *Culburra*, 26 August 1918; *Challamba*, 2 October 1918; *Coolcha* 26 October 1918. A further contract had been signed for the building of ten wooden steamers with the Oregon company, the Patterson McDonald Shipbuilding Co., but only one ship was delivered before the war ended. This was *Bellata* on 8 October 1918. Then followed *Bundarra*, 11 December 1918; *Bethanga*, 5 May 1919; *Birriwa*, 6 August 1919. It was then decided that the remaining ships under construction be diesel powered. Of these vessels *Benowa* was delivered on 15 June 1919 and *Babinda* on 5 August 1919. This left three ships uncompleted:- *Balcatta, Boobyalla* and *Borrika*. As a result of hasty construction and unseasoned materials, the ships that had entered service proved most unsatisfactory. In my research I have not come across anything printed in their favour. The Australian Government decided to cut their losses. Nine of the ships, including the three uncompleted hulls, were sold at bargain rates to American buyers. The sale was finalised on 2 September 1919. The Commonwealth Line was left with *Bundarra, Bellata, Bethanga, Birriwa* and *Birringa,* all steamships. These ships were also sold to American buyers on 3 October 1919, less than fifteen months after delivery of *Cethana,* the first of the fourteen. This should have closed an unhappy chapter of the history of the Commonwealth Line, but it was not to be. The American buyers of the five steamers defaulted; in brief, Australia was stuck with them. For a few months, between periods of laying up for repairs, the five ships were engaged in the Australian coastal trade. I quote some of their movements and cargoes during that period.

December 1920: *Bellata* at Sydney waiting for crew for voyage to Rabaul and Kavieng to load copra for Sydney.

Berringa discharging timber at Melbourne, then in ballast to Newcastle to load coal for Melbourne. A.U.S.N.Co. Agents.

Birriwa arrived Melbourne with timber from Cairns. Future business not yet fixed. A.U.S.N. Co. Agents.

Bundarra arrived Brisbane 27 December, due to sail 31 December for Sydney. Future business not yet fixed. Adelaide Steamship Co. Agents.

Bethanga arrived Port Pirie 24 December with coke from Port Kembla. On discharge loads concentrates to Newcastle. Howard Smith & Co. Agents.

March 1921 saw *Bellata* loading coke in Sydney for discharge at Port Alma, Rockhampton's deepwater Port. One wonders what Rockhampton did with a ship load of coke. It could have been for the fleet of coke fired steam trams which were a feature of the city for many years. Coal, coke, timber and concentrates seem to have been the main cargoes of the wooden ships in their brief period on the Australian coastal trade. They visited all ports from Bunbury in the west to Cairns in the north in their quest for cargoes, and when these were no longer available, were left to rot. In 1923 the Federal Parliament passed legislation to reconstitute the Australian Commonwealth Line. During the debate, the Prime Minister (Mr S.M. Bruce) had this to say regarding the heavy financial loss of the American wooden ship purchase:- "The wooden tonnage had nothing to do with the operations of the Commonwealth Line as such. Those wooden vessels were built as a direct war measure on the responsiblity of the Government; their capital cost and the losses in their operations constituted a war enterprise that must be regarded as quite apart from the Commonwealth Shipping Line". A fair epilogue for this segment of the Commonwealth Line.

Chapter 8

THE "D" AND "E" CLASS SHIPS

The "D" class steel cargo ships were identical with the 'E" class ships built during the four years following the commissioning of the "D" class. A brief description of these standardised ships is as follows:-

Built on the longitudinal system of framing invented by J.W. Isherwood, their dimensions were — length 331 feet, breadth 48 feet, moulded depth 26 feet 1 inch, and a deadweight capacity of 5,500 tons, on a draft of 21 feet 8 inches. The ships were propelled by triple expansion three cylinder engines (25 inch, 41 inch and 68 inch by 45 inch stroke), with boilers designed for 180 lbs., pressure, to develop 2,300 indicated horse power, the single cast iron propeller doing 75 revolutions per minute for the ship to steam at 10½ knots.

Steel plates for the construction of these 6 ships were in short supply, and some were imported from America. Fittings etc. imported from England were cables, wire ropes, compass outfits, signal lamps, joiners' hardware, side lights, steering chains and electric wiring. Other fittings of the hulls and superstructures were made in Australia.

The first of the "D" class, *Dromana,* was laid down at Williamstown on 3 May 1918. It was anticipated that *Dromana* would be launched in January, 1919, but it was 11 May, 1919 before she slid gracefully into Hobson's Bay. Work on the ship must have been well advanced prior to the launching, for she was delivered to her owners on 27 August 1919. The engines for *Dromana* were built by Messrs Thompson & Co. at Castlemaine, Victoria. The Commonwealth Ship Construction branch of Williamstown must have learned a lot by trial and error on *Dromana*. Their next construction, *Dumosa,* was launched 25 November 1919 and put into service on 8 March 1920. Meanwhile, at Walsh Island, three more

"D" class ships were under construction by the New South Wales Government. *Delungra* was launched on 25 March 1919, delivery being made on 30 October 1919. *Dinoga's* launching took place on 17 October 1919. There was some delay at the fitting out berth, for she was not completed till 12 December, 1920. The remaining ship of the Newcastle trio, *Dilga* was more fortunate; launched on 15 November 1919, she sailed with her first cargo on 15 May 1920. The last of the "D" class, *Dundula* was constructed by the Commonwealth Navy Department at Cockatoo Island. Sydney did fairly well by launching *Dundula* on 9 July 1919 and having her in service on 28 April 1920. *Dundula's* engines, however, were manufactured in the Victorian country town of Castlemaine by Messrs Thompson & Co. The engines for the Newcastle ships were made by the ships' builders, the New South Wales Government dockyards. By the end of 1920 the six "D" class ships were hard at work, carrying Australia's produce to the Dutch East Indies and beyond. This trade had already been started by the ex-German units of the Commonwealth Line. *Dilga's* voyage commenced at Newcastle, loading also at Sydney, Melbourne, Adelaide and Fremantle for Batavia, Samarang, and Sourabaya and *Dilga* proceeded to Ocean Island to load phosphates for Australia. The voyages of *Dinoga* and *Dromana* followed the same route. The three ships only made a few overseas voyages. They were not profitable, having a small bunker capacity. They had to replenish their coal supplies at a high cost in Batavia. *Dumosa* was placed on the ironstone and coal run between Whyalla and Newcastle, with Howard Smith Ltd. as agents. *Dundula* also worked on the same route under the agency of the Melbourne Steamship Co. *Delungra* was assigned to the Newcastle—Port Pirie coal and concentrates trade. By 1922 the Australia — Java — Ocean Island run was abandoned and the ships engaged thereon took their place on the coastal trade. *Dinoga's* life history before she ended up at the Foochow shipbreakers in 1959 was a varied one under various names. She was purchased by Huddart Parker in 1925 and re-named *Colac*. She voyaged along the Southern and Western coasts of Australia until 1952. Purchased by James Paterson & Co. and re-named *Easby* for their Sydney and Melbourne trade, her hard worked engines broke down and *Easby* was eventually towed into Sydney by the tug *St. Giles*. In 1956 *Easby*, ex *Dinoga*, loaded coal at Newcastle for Hong Kong, having been sold to the Chinese firm Cambay Prince Steamship Co. She sailed via Darwin under the name of *Clyde Breeze*. Another change of ownership to the firm of Wallen & Co. of Panama, under her former name *Easby* came about in 1959. A few months later she sailed to the Republic of China and the ship breakers.

Dumosa was sold out of the Commonwealth Line in 1923 and from then to 1952 sailed under the flag of James Paterson & Co. of Melbourne. On completion of 30 years hard slogging through the Bass Straits, *Dumosa* went east, following the track of aged Australian coasters, no longer A.1 at Lloyds, but good for years of service in the Far East where regulations were few and safety standards minimal. *Dromana* was sold in 1924 to Howard Smith's. The remaining "D" class ships carried on with the Commonwealth Line until 1926 and were then sold to join the expanding fleets of the Australian Coastal Companies. The six ships were a credit to their builders and served their various owners well.

The "E" Class Ships

The original programme of building called for the building of 24 "D" and "E" Class cargo vessels. The contracts were allotted as follows:-

Commonwealth Ship Construction Branch, Williamstown	6
New South Wales Government, Walsh Island, Newcastle	6
Commonwealth Navy Department, Cockatoo Island, Sydney	2
Walkers Ltd., Maryborough, Queensland	4
Poole & Steel, Adelaide	4
Mersey Shipbuilding Co. Ltd., Tasmania	2

Within a few months this programme was drastically pruned. Although costly expansion was made to the Tasmanian Shipyard of the Mersey Shipbuilding Co., the contract for the building of their quota of "E" class ships was cancelled before construction was started. Later, Adelaide's contract was reduced from four to three and Walkers of Queensland received similar treatment. The actual building programme for the building of the "E" class ships was:-

Commonwealth Navy Dept., Sydney (1) *Eudunda*

New South Wales Government, Newcastle (3) *Eurelia, Enoggera, Eromanga*

Commonwealth Ship Construction Branch, Williamstown (4) *Emita, Erriba, Euroa, Elouera*

Walkers Ltd , Queensland (2) *Echuca, Echunga*

Poole & Steel, Adelaide (3) *Euwarra, Erina,* and *Eurimbla.*

There appears to have been some duplication in the naming of *Erina*. Quite early in her career, she was re-named *Eugowra*. The main improvement of the "E" class was their deadweight capacity of 6,170 cubic feet, compared with the 5,608 feet of the "D" Class. Otherwise, their dimensions, net and gross tonnages were identical. Some of the ships had pole derricks, others lattice derricks. As the "E" Class ships were completed and handed over to the Commonwealth Line, the owners found increasing difficulty in securing cargoes for them. A brief extract from the balance sheets tells its own story.

Profit on the line's working

	Profit
From 16 Oct. 1916 to 30 June 1918	£ 903,500
From 1 July 1918 to 30 June 1919	£1,160,034
From 1 July 1919 to 30 June 1920	£ 137,959
From 1 July 1920 to 30 June 1921	£ 102,949
Total Profit	£2,304,442

As the last of the "E" class ships were being delivered, profits ceased to exist and huge losses took their place.

From 1 July 1921 to 30 June 1922 the gross earnings of the fleet were £2,274,204 whilst gross expenditure was £3,445,773. Net loss for the year: £1,171,569. The figures for 1922-23 were even worse; earnings were £2,529,800; expenditure (plus interest and depreciation) £4,155,959; net loss £1,626,159. Even while ships were laid up, expenses still went on. One item on the balance sheet for 1922-23 was: Expenses of Lay Up £55,223.12s.8d.

Having digressed somewhat, I shall revert to the story of the well built, but unwanted "E" class ships. *Eudunda*, the first, was launched on 29 March 1920, and *Erina*, launched on 4 November 1922 was the last.

Eurelia, launched on 10 April 1920, was the first to be completed, being delivered to the Commonwealth Line on 21 December 1920. She was placed on the Newcastle-Adelaide coal trade under the agency of McIlwraith McEacharn; *Eurelia* was registered at Adelaide. She was sold to the A.U.S.N. Co. in 1926, and served that company well as *Mungana* until 1951, when she was sold to Eastern buyers. *Enoggera*, registered at Brisbane, left Newcastle with her first cargo in February 1921. She also joined the fleet of the A.U.S.N. Co. in 1924; re-named *Mildura*, she carried all varieties of cargo around the Australian coast until 1956. She was then taken over by eastern buyers, and a few months later was lost off the China coast during a typhoon. *Emita*, registered at Hobart, was delivered in time to take her place on the Batavia-Singapore service; she left on her first voyage on 29 April 1921. By the end of the year she was back on the Australian coastal service. *Emita* was sold to the A.U.S.N. Co. in 1926, as *Milora*, She only had a comparatively short life, being wrecked at the entrace of Port Phillip Bay on 21 September 1934. Even the notorious "Rip" could not finish the staunch *Milora*. She was eventually salvaged, but as the hull was badly strained and there was plenty of surplus tonnage in those depression years, it was decided to take off all metal and fittings of value. This having been done, *Milora* was towed out to sea and sunk. Several years before this *Milora* had grounded at the "Devil's Elbow", a sharp bend in the Fitzroy River, a mile downstream from the Port of Rockhampton; three weeks of time and the assistance of Brisbane tugs enabled *Milora* to get clear and resume her interrupted voyage. *Elouera*, launched on 2 March 1922 and completed a year later, saw little service with the Commonwealth Line. In 1925 she was bought by the Broken Hill Pty. Ltd., for their coal and ore trade and renamed *Iron Prince*. After 30 years service she was sold to Manners, a Hong Kong shipping firm, and sailed on under the name of *Kembla Breeze*. In 1959 she made her final voyage to the Hong Kong scrap yards.

Eudunda registered at Sydney and launched on 29 March 1920 does not appear in the 1920 sailing lists. She was under coastal charter for a period in 1921, then had several lengthy lay ups, until sold to the firm of Burns, Philip & Co. in 1926. It was the practice of this firm to name their ships with seven letter names commencing with the latter "M", such as *Montoro, Marella*, etc. *Eudunda* was given the name *Mangola* and placed on the Pacific Islands run. At the age of 37, she was sold to the Manners Steamship Co. of Hong Kong, re-named *Torres Breeze*, finally passing on to the Hong Kong shipbreakers at the ripe old age of 40.

Studying the history of these ships, one is impressed not only with their ruggedness and years of service, but at the price at which they were sold to Eastern buyers. In each case, the figure was around £140,000. Getting 30 odd years of continuous service and then selling them for a sum in excess of their book value in 1925 can be regarded as a little known tribute to Australian ship building. *Eurimbla* launched at Adelaide on 24 April and completed too late for the post war shipping boom, was sold in 1924, to the Broken Hill Steel Company and sailed under the name of *Iron Master*. Thirty five years later, after having hauled countless tons of coal and iron ore along the southern and eastern coasts of Australia, *Iron Master* ex *Eurimbla* sailed to Hong Kong and the shipbreakers.

Echuca, launched at Maryborough, Queensland on 6 June 1921, was the largest ship ever built in Queensland to that date. The task of launching such a large vessel into the narrow confines of the Mary River, called for precise calculation and timing. *Echuca* only made a few voyages for the Commonwealth Line and passed to the ownership of the A.U.S.N. Co. in 1924, being renamed *Mareeba*. . She served on the Adelaide-Rockhampton general cargo service for a number of years. Her first overseas voyage was also her last. *Mareeba* left Fremantle on 13 May 1941 with a full cargo of flour. After calling at Singapore, she sailed for Colombo. A few days later she was intercepted by the German raider *Kormoran;* after taking off the crew, the raider gave *Mareeba* a full broadside with her six inch guns. This failed to sink the ship, so well built by the craftsmen of Maryborough. *Kormoran* had to use her precious torpedoes, before *Mareeba* sank stern first into the depths of the Indian Ocean. A relic of *Mareeba* ex *Echuca* rests in the Australian War Memorial. During their period on the German raider, *Mareeba's* crew managed to seal messages in bottles and drop them overboard in the forlorn hope they would give warning of the raider's presence. One of these signed by *Mareeba's* Master (Captain Skinner) was picked up on the beach at Yanchep, Western Australia in December 1945. The bottle and message was donated to the Australian War Memorial by the Editor of the Perth Daily News. A few yards from this sad relic is a shell torn Carley float, all that is left of the Australian cruiser *Sydney*, which sank after a battle with the *Kormoran* on 19 November 1941. In the courtyard of the Memorial are the names of the 645 officers and ratings of the *Sydney* who went down with their ship. *Kormoran* was later abandoned, before sinking, as a result of the Sydney's shelling. Captain Skinner lost his life in February 1942, when a German prison ship to which *Mareeba's* crew had been transferred, was torpedoed and sunk off the Azores. As *Mareeba* left Fremantle Harbour on her final voyage, H.M.A.S. *Sydney* was entering the port. *Mareeba's* red ensign was 'dipped' in salute. *Sydney's* white ensign was lowered in return. Each ship went on their lawful occasions, later to meet their fate by the same enemy warship.

Erriba launched on 10 December 1920 was another late arrival to the fleet of the Commonwealth Line. Her name appears infrequently on the 1922-23 sailings and she seems to have spent longer awaiting cargoes than in carrying them, until 1925 when she joined the fleet of the A.U.S.N. Co. as *Murada*. She had a busy but unspectacular life in the Australian Coastal trade, surviving World War 2, and was sold to Eastern buyers in the early 1950's. *Euroa*, launched on 27 January 1922, and completed at the Williamstown fitting out berth ten months later, spent some months moored in Hobsons Bay, waiting for better times, and a change of fortune for the Commonwealth Line. Neither of these eventuated, and in 1926 Euroa joined the Broken Hill Fleet and became the *Iron Crown*, to spend a good deal of her life under a pall of coal and iron ore dust, doing 30 years hard labour, before voyaging to the east to carry scrap iron to rebuild the Japanese empire.

Euwarra, launched on 17 December 1921, was fortunate enough to pick up some charter voyages with Howard Smith's, before joining her sister ships in the Broken Hill Pty. Fleet. Her new name *Iron Knob* lacked the dignity of those given to the other ships — *Iron Crown, Iron Prince, Iron Master* and *Iron Warrior*. *Euwarra* was named after the town of Iron Knob, which the gazetteer describes as a South Australian town, connected by rail to Whyalla, noted for iron ore and with a population of 628 people. Like the other ex-Commonwealth Line Ships *Iron Knob* played her part in building up Australia's industries, before losing her identity "out east".

Eurelia, launched on 10 May 1920, and registered at Adelaide, also found her way into the coal trade under the agency of McIlwraith McEacharn. Her voyages from Newcastle to Albany in Western Australia averaged 8 days. Some general cargo was carried in the 'tween decks on these occasions. Her first voyage scheduled for 21st December 1920 was delayed by crew troubles; perhaps the crew could think of better place to spend Christmas than in the Great Australian Bight.

The Newcastle-Western Australian run was quite a profitable one. The ships carried full cargoes of coal westward and on the return voyage carried jarrah sleepers for the ever-expanding railways of Victoria and New South Wales. *Eurelia* was sold to the A.U.S.N. Co. in 1926 to become *Mungana.* Throughout the depression years, *Mungana* and her consorts carried their loads of cement, building materials and all other cargoes around the Australian coasts. Coastal shipping freights were so low, road or rail could not compete. *Mungana* remained on the coastal trade until 1952, before going to Hong Kong registry.

Eromanga, launched on 12 March 1921 and delivered to the Commonwealth Line ten months later, followed the well used routes of the coal trade: Newcastle, Melbourne and Adelaide, and in 1926 joined the A.U.S.N. Co. as *Maranoa.* This Company made some improvements to the six ships they purchased from the Commonwealth Line. These were mainly to speed up cargo handling. Samson posts and derricks were erected at the forepart of No. 1 hatch, the afterpart of No. 2 hatch, and the forepart of No. 3 hatch, with an extra pair of winches at three of the four hatches. This enabled the employment of seven gangs of waterside workers instead of four; in addition to these, a gang could also be engaged "passing out" through doors in the ships side leading into the 'tween deck. On the general cargo run, the Adelaide, Geelong, Melbourne, Sydney, Newcastle, Brisbane, Rockhampton weekly schedule, the round voyage was accomplished in four weeks and was designed to spend each Sunday at sea. During the four week trip, bunkers were filled whilst loading steel products at Newcastle. I recall the cluttered state of the decks while these ships were in port; the fourteen winches took up much of the deck space, and what was left appeared to be a jumble of hatch boards, fore and aft and athwartship hatch beams inter-laced with mooring wires and cargo handing impedimenta. *Maranoa* was sold in 1935. The A.U.S.N. Co. planned to modernise its fleet and shortly afterwards took delivery of the new motor vessel *Corinda..*

Echunga, the second of Maryborough's contributions to the fleet of the Commonwealth Line, was launched on 14 December 1921 and, on completion, spent a period of laying up at Williamstown. Shortly afterwards she was sold to Interstate Steamships. *Echunga* was the only one of the "E" class to retain her original name. She sailed around the Australian coasts until April 1957 when the Panamanian Oriental Steamship Co. of Panama purchased her for the sum of £144,000. From then on the change of names and ownership were confusing enough to thwart any research in to her subsequent movements.

Eugowra launched as *Erina* on 4 November 1922 was accepted by the Commonwealth Line in June 1923, but did not appear to have many voyages under their ownership. She made a few charter voyages for the ever expanding Broken Hill Company and passed to their ownership in 1926, taking the name of *Iron Warrior* to become a well known part of the busy Newcastle waterfront scene. Time, and more modern ships with their improved crew accommodation, made the older vessels obsolete. *Iron Warrior* ex *Eugowra* ex *Erina* left Newcastle in 1956 with a load of scrap metal for the blast furnaces of Japan, then to continue her coal and iron ore voyages around the Manchurian Coast.

A summary of the D and E class ships is one of failure to accomplish what they were built for; this is the debit side of the ledger. The credit side is much brighter. They lived a long and useful life serving Australia under private ownership. They required little maintenance, thus keeping freight charges low. They were also capable of using the existing wharves of the various ports, required no special docking facilities and above all, survived millions of miles of steaming through Bass Strait gales, Queensland cyclones and the fury of the Great Australian Bight.

Chapter 9

THE BAY SHIPS

Many people, both laymen and seafarers, with whom I have discussed the Australian Commonwealth Line, have said "Yes, I know about the ships, the five Bays and the two Dales". Seven ships only remembered, out of seventy which had sailed under the flag of the Australian Government. It is true that by 1926 the seven ships were all that remained. The shipping line had become a political football in 1923 with the change in the Federal Government. The Bays and Dales had their part to play, even though they came in rather late in the day. I have, in an earlier chapter, given a brief portrayal of these ships and perhaps this should be enlarged upon.

Moreton Bay, *Hobsons Bay* and *Jervis Bay* were built by Vickers of Barrow in Furness. *Largs Bay* and *Esperance Bay* were Clyde built by Wm Beardmore and Company. Tonnage and other measurements have already been given, but to show the careful designing and planning of the five ships, a few more details will not go amiss.

The naming of the ships was planned to overcome the traditional jealousies of the five States of the Commonwealth, the Northern Territory being excluded as remote, and Tasmania alone to the south, usually referred to as "The Speck", as not belonging to the Australian Mainland. *Esperance Bay* was named after a remote stretch of water on the south coast of Western Australia, *Largs Bay* after a small bay near Adelaide. Victoria was honoured with *Hobsons Bay* in the harbour of Port Phillip; New South Wales with *Jervis Bay*, a harbour a hundred miles south of Sydney, frequented by ships of the Royal Australian Navy. Finally Queensland was remembered by *Moreton Bay* at the approaches to Brisbane. Moreton Island, which separates the Bay from the Ocean, is noted for Mount Tempest, 914 feet in height and the highest known sand dune in the World. The ships were not built for cheapness. Materials used were of top quality. Twin screw, each shaft driven through double reduction gearing by two Parsons compound turbines, the four bladed propellers were made of manganese bronze. The standard horse power of 9,000 gave the ships a speed of 14 knots, the propellers turning at 90 revolutions per minute. Five boilers, three double ended and two single ended, were installed in the boiler room. These consumed oil fuel at the rate of 90 tons per day. The capacity of the bunkers was 3,413 tons of oil. The boilers and bunkers were designed for coal as an alternative to oil, but coal was never used. Two motor boats and twelve life boats were carried; half of these were 28 feet long and were stowed in the larger ones which were 30 feet long. The colour of the hulls of the ships of the Commonwealth Government Line was all grey; with the Bay Ships it was decided that the colour of the hulls be black, with a white superstructure and a yellow funnel. They were comfortable ships to travel on for cargo-passenger liners. They had none of the glamour of the present day cruise ships, but the standard of victualling was quite good. Many of today's Australians had their first glimpse of Terra Australis from the decks of the Bay ships. Brisbane was the terminal port, where the ships berthed at New Farm Wharf, a two mile tram ride from the centre of the city.

For many years, passengers wishing to travel by sea along the Australian Coasts had been well catered for by various local shipping companies. Between them, a service unequalled anywhere else in the World was maintained. In return for this, competition from overseas ships was not allowed, either with cargo or passengers. An exception was made with the Bay ships. They were permitted to carry coastal passengers. However, the comfort and good service of the Australian coastal ships was hard to compete with, and the Bay ships carried only a few interstate passengers. Rail and air competition caused the abandonment of the Australian coastal passenger services in the 1950's. Today the few interstate passengers remaining loyal to the sea routes are allowed to travel on any ship of any nationality which will take them. The Bay ships were typical of the passenger cargo liners once so common, now so few. Shipping companies have realised the impossibility of maintaining a schedule with the vagaries of waterside cargo handling conditions. In the days before air conditioning reached its present state of efficiency, inside cabins, or those well down in the ship where port holes could not be opened, were not wanted by full fare paying passengers. With migrants who were just allotted to the ship and had no selection of accommodation, it was a case of "Hobsons Choice". Having broken the links with home, they had to make the best of it, though the dismal stifling six and eight berth cabins looked nothing like the illustrations in the glossy brochures they had seen in the Travel bureaus. In the passenger-cargo liners, much of the centre portion of the ship was taken up by hatchways and cargo holds. With the introduction of air conditioning and fluorescent lighting these types of ships were remodelled and former cargo spaces given over to passenger cabins and amenities.

The migrant ships from Britain carried many more passengers outward to Australia than they did on the return voyage. This was done by using 'tween deck cargo spaces, austerely fitted for passenger transport. This meant that more staff were required in the catering section outward bound, whose services could not be used on the homeward voyage. This difficulty was overcome by the acceptance of passage workers, who, on arrival in Sydney, were paid off. The rate of pay was nominal, one shilling per month. This sum had to be paid in order that the temporary crew be signed on the ship's articles, and thus be under the Master's command and subject to his discipline. These passage workers usually unskilled, lived the sunless existence of troglodytes, in the ship's galleys, pantries, and storerooms. Washing up, referred to as "pearl diving" took up a great deal of their day, the remaining time being spent mopping out corridors and ablution places.

The ships permanent scullery men and pantry men worked the outward trip as trainee cooks and stewards. The Bay ships could not take advantage of this free labour; the Australian Unions made it very clear what would happen to the ships if passage workers were carried. So larger crews were signed on, with little to do for the six week duration of the northbound voyage.

Passage workers made up quite a significant part of Australia's migrants. The cost of an adult assisted passage in the 1920's was £33, of which the passenger paid £11, the British and Commonwealth Governments sharing equally the other two thirds. Having arrived in Australia, the passage worker had reached the point of no return, with his two shillings pay for the voyage. He was on his own with no benevolent migration officer to give him a railway ticket and the advice to "go west young man, go west". It was impossible to work a passage back to Britain and stowaways were anathema to ships' captains of any nationality. So the only thing the passage worker could do was to get a job and, if ties with the homeland were still strong, save enough money for his passage. In the lengthy interval this would take, he became an Australian and could find better use for his savings. The professional seafarer, who by some mischance found himself stranded on some foreign shore, could locate the nearest shipping master or British Consul and apply for a passage as "a distressed British seaman", always abbreviated to "D.B.S." Having convinced the authorities of his *bona fides,* a passage was arranged for him on any British bound ship with a spare bunk in the crew's quarters. He was expected to work but compulsion could not be used. The ship's owners were not paid for the passage, hence the lack of V.I.P. Treatment.

The crews of the Bay ships were not noted for their servility and soon put awkward passengers in their place. The ships were well patronised by Australians; they had a proprietary interest in them. Another big advantage was the fact that they went to all the States except Tasmania to embark and disembark passengers. Nearly twenty years have passed since the last of the Bay ships departed from Australia, her five ton anchor dropped for the last time and the bridge telegraph rung down to the engine room "Finished with Engines". It is sad to view a ship at the breaker's yard; there is something obscene in the yawning gaps in the deck and the gangs of workers tearing away at the ships vitals. Four of the "Bay" ships went that way. *Jervis Bay* found her resting place in the depths of the North Atlantic — she went down with colours flying. Being an incurable romantic regarding ships, I would spare them from the indignity of the scrap yard. When the time came for Australia's flagship, the 19,200 ton battle cruiser *Australia* to die on 12 April 1924, she was towed 25 miles out of Sydney Heads, accompanied by other ships of the Australian Navy. As the demolition charges were detonated and *Australia* sank stern first into the Pacific a twenty-one gun salute was fired by the accompanying cruisers and destroyers. The "Bay" ships deserved a similar fate.

I have, in this chapter, referred to the Australian coastal passenger fleets. Chapter 10 contains a description of s.s. *Indarra*, the ultimate in Australian Coastal passenger liners and also a short survey of the pre-First World War period when the Australian coastal fleets were at their peak, both in tonnage and efficiency.

Chapter 10

AUSTRALIA'S LARGEST COASTAL SHIP

The s.s. *Indarra*, built by Wm. Denny and Brothers of Dumbarton in 1910, was by far the largest and most commodious vessel ever designed for the Australian coastal trade. She was constructed for the requirements of the A.U.S.N. Co., designed especially for their Melbourne — Fremantle service. This was not a "Sheltered Water" route; the Great Australian Bight, like its counterpart in the Northern Hemisphere, the Bay of Biscay has a well earned reputation for high seas, and consequent discomfort, amongst world travellers. With gold discoveries in Western Australia a huge demand for passages came from fortune hunters in the eastern states of Australia. The A.U.S.N. commenced a service linking Sydney, Melbourne, Adelaide and Fremantle, using two ships *Pilbarra* and *Paroo* each of 2,700 tons. These proved to be too small; furthermore they lacked the comfort and amenities of the P. & O. Orient liners of that time, with which they had to compete. In 1903 *Kyarra* and *Kanowna*, newly built for the A.U.S.N. Co., took over the run to the west from the smaller ships. *Kyarra* and *Kanowna* were sister ships, of 5,300 horse power and 6,950 tons net. They carried 3 classes of passengers, 1st class, 2nd class and steerage, fares from Sydney to Fremantle, being £10, £7, £5 respectively. Passenger accommodation was mainly in the superstructure, leaving the hull space for general cargo.

Within a few years *Indarra* was planned for a four weekly service to the West, thus enabling *Kanowna* and *Kyarra* to continue their good work on the expanding Melbourne to Cairns service. No expense was spared in the building and fitting out of *Indarra*, constructed to Lloyds' highest standards, 100A1. She was a twin screw vessel of 7,734 tons (net), 450 feet in length, with a breadth of 60 feet. Her engines were duplicate sets of quadruple expansion, designed for a speed of 15 knots. The passengers were accommodated on seven decks, five of these being above the main deck.

Two tall masts and two funnels completed the graceful appearance of this ship, the Queen of Australia's Coastal Fleet. Accommodation was provided for 490 passengers, 230 first class in one, two and three berth cabins, 140 second class, and 120 Third Class. In the Edwardian era, public rooms on the ocean liners were built and furnished in a baronial manor style, plenty of oak panelling, huge mock fireplaces, lofty ceilings with domes of stained glass. The first class dining saloon, smoke room and drawing room on *Indarra* excelled in opulence those of the recently launched *Mauretania* and *Lusitania*. It would seem that shipowners of those days tried to make their passengers forget they were at sea. *Indarra's* drawing room with its lofty plaster ceilings, intricately moulded designs, doric columns and grand piano, looked like a transplant from the London Savoy Hotel. The smoke room had an oak beamed ceiling in the centre of which was a glass dome decorated with coloured replicas from the days of sail. An indoor swimming pool, the first ever built on an Australian Coaster, catered for the more athletic type of passenger. Sufficient lifeboats were provided for twice the number of passengers and crew *Indarra* normally carried. It was only after the *Titanic* disaster and the subsequent inquiry several years after *Indarra's* launching, that such provision became mandatory under international law. When a ship is sinking, she is very seldom on an even keel, making the launching of all lifeboats a hazardous proceeding. Lifeboat stowage and launching davits had not altered for over a hundred years, requiring much muscle power and good teamwork to get them out of their chocks on the Boat Deck and safely over the side into the water. A ship on fire or sinking was usually a scene of chaos, and the desired teamwork and precision lacking. An entirely new innovation was made with *Indarra's* lifeboats; they were stowed high over the rails of the boat deck ready for a speedy launching. Electric motors were there to save manpower. All this meant more deck space for recreation and organised games, and is now standard in all passenger ships. *Indarra* was one of the first ships to be designed in such manner and she was well ahead of the European Transatlantic Liners of her day. The seven decks were serviced by a lift which held six passengers, another first on the Australian Coast.

With all this solid comfort and luxury, the cost of a 1st class passage of £15 return from Sydney to Fremantle, a voyage of 4,900 nautical miles, was excellent value. The menus, cooking and steward service equalled that of the P. & O. Line; in the various ports passengers could invite guests aboard for meals, at a cost of 2s.6d. It was fashionable for doctors to prescribe a sea trip for their patients. A.U.S.N. Co. provided this in well found ships, from Fremantle to Burketown, a distance of 5,040 nautical miles, calling at 17 interesting Ports for the sum of £25 5s.0d. First Class, £12.5s.0d steerage. For several years *Indarra* played her part in developing the West and then came 1914, and the beginning of a war that meant the end of an era. Amongst many other ships of the Australian Coast Fleet, the large A.U.N.S. Liners were taken over by the Admiralty and they bore the proud title H.M.S. *Indarra* sailed as a troop ship and her voyages covered most ports of the world. On her return to Australia in 1919, no place could be found for her on the coastal trade. The trans-continental Railway now linked the East and the West, and sea travellers were catered for by the ships of Huddart Parker. *Indarra* was under charter to the Orient Line for a while and, in 1920 was sold to the Belgian Government. Later she passed into the hands of Japanese owners and sailed on through the years as *Horai Maru*. She failed to survive World War II, for her name was not on the post war listings. *Kyarra* served as a Hospital Ship and was torpedoed off the English Coast in May 1918. *Kanowna* also had distinguished service as a Hospital Ship, survived the war and returned to the Eastern Australian coastal service. She was wrecked on Cleft Island on 17 February 1929. Like *Indarra*, the history of the A.U.S.N. Co. was only a brief one measured in time, but one can only admire the courage, enterprise and, above all, the confidence they showed in the future of Australia, by building such a fleet of ships, which did so much to develop Australia.

The headquarters of this company were in Mary Street, Brisbane. It is still one of Brisbane's distinguished buildings, light, cool and airy, built for the City's torrid summer climate, patterned on the offices of British India Line in Calcutta, and is sometimes referred to, somewhat facetiously, as the Taj Mahal.

Chapter 11

THE DALE SHIPS

Ferndale and *Fordsdale,* laid down in 1922 and launched in 1924, broke all records in Australian shipbuilding. They were the largest ships ever built in

Australia, a record that was to remain intact until the bulk carrier *Iron Wyndham* was launched at Whyalla in 1952. This ship was four and a half feet longer than the Dales and three feet wider, but her gross tonnage was 1,563 tons less than the orthodox general cargo carriers launched thirty years earlier. The "Dale" ships also had the largest reciprocating engines ever built in Australia, a record that stands intact to this day and, in this age of motorships, is never likely to be broken.

As this is primarily a history, a full description of these sister ships in warranted. As with all the other Australian built ships, the standards of construction were very high. The crew accommodation, both in comfort and space, was far ahead of anything provided in other ships. The "Dales" were designed to carry all types of cargo, having twelve sets of derricks, including the "jumbo" for heavy lifts on the after side of the foremast. A good proportion of the cargo space was fitted to carry refrigerated produce. The ships were twin screw, propelled by two sets of quadruple expansion steam reciprocating engines; the balancing of these was on Yarrow-Schlick and Tweedie systems. The cylinders were 24 inches, 30 inches, 48½ inches, and 70 inches respectively, with a 54 inch stroke, and the two sets of engines gave a total of 11,000 indicated horse power. The six boilers in each of the ships were also built at Cockatoo Dockyard in Sydney. The ships were coal fired; each boiler had four corrugated furnaces fitted with the Howdens forced draught system. The gross tonnage of each ship was 11,023, net tonnage, 6,741. The total length of 500 feet included the raised forecastle of 85 feet and a shelter deck amidships. It was quite an achievement building such ships in the difficult economy of the post war years of 1922 and 1924.

The launchings went smoothly and were witnessed by thousands of onlookers. It is certainly a spectacular sight and an anxious time for all those responsible for the construction when ten thousand tons of steel which has been part of the landscape for months is set in motion to go gliding down the launching ways. As the ship becomes waterborne, the bow dips as if in salute to those who designed and fabricated her. The successful launching of a ship is the final solution to a host of converging problems, and proof that the mathematician has done his work well. This colourful method of getting a steel collosus from land to water is becoming obsolete. Ships are now built in dry docks. After the speeches, the blessing and the breaking of the traditional bottle of champagne, nothing dramatic takes place. Behind the scenes, a valve is turned and a trickle of water appears on the floor of the dock. Hours later when the official party and spectators have gone their various ways, enough water is in the dock to lift the ship off the blocks. This dry dock method is a revival of an old idea. Brunels' masterpiece the *Great Britian* was built in similar fashion at Bristol in 1843. She also had the distinction of being launched by Prince Albert. Cockatoo Island has reason to be proud of *Fordsdale* and *Ferndale*; engines, boilers and the ships themselves performed well. Their speed of 15½ knots, slightly more than that of the Bay ships, put them in the express cargo ship class. There are no separate figures for profitability or otherwise of the two ships; their initial cost was high owing to the relatively high wage structure in Australia. This would be a handicap in assessing profits on a large capital outlay. Two more ships of the same class were planned but later deferred as overseas competition increased. The "Dale" ships carried large cargoes; *Ferndale* broke another record in May, 1927 when she arrived in Australia with 10,239 tons of cargo, the largest tonnage ever to reach Australia in one ship. *Ferndale's* short but useful life finished in 1928 when she ran ashore on the North African Coast and became a total loss. With the disposal of the Commonwealth Shipping Line, *Fordsdale* remained on the United Kingdom-Australasia trade under the flag of the Shaw Savill and Albion Line until 1953, when she was sold to Hong Kong buyers.

Chapter 12

MIGRATION

The Commonwealth Government Shipping Line was controlled from Australia House, London, for several years after the Line's formation. The General Manager was Mr H.B.G. Larkin, Assistant Manager, Mr G.H. Kneen. The Australian Office was at 447 Collins Street, Melbourne, under the management of Mr E.A. Eva with Mr S.A. Nosgood as traffic superintendent. The ex-German ships had been placed under the management of the Line, some for only short periods with others taking their place. The year 1923 saw a drastic pruning in the number of ships and the title of the line altered to the Australian Commonwealth Line. The Commonwealth Shipping Act 1923 provided for the establishment of the Australian Commonwealth Line of Steamers under the control of a Board of Directors consisting of not less than three, nor more than five members. The date at which the Act was to come into force was fixed by proclamation at 1 September 1923. The whole of the right, title and interest of the Commonwealth in and to the 50 vessels (155,302 tons net) of the Commonwealth Government Line of Steamers, and appurtenances used for the purpose of such vessels, were vested in the Board, also four other vessels (15,442 tons net) which were under construction at the time of transfer. The valuation of the vessels, tackle, apparel, gear, furniture, stores and equipment was fixed at £4,718,150, office furniture and fittings at £7,500, and stores on hand £23,700, making a total of £4,749,350.

The operation of the Commonwealth Government Line of steamers revealed profits on working as follows:-

16th October 1916	to 30th June 1918	£ 903,500
1st July 1918	to 30th June 1919	£1,160,034
1st July, 1919	to 30th June 1920	£ 137,959
1st July, 1920	to 30th June 1921	£ 102,949

This was the end of the period of profitability for the Line. For the year ending 30 June 1922, the gross earnings of the fleet were £2,274,204, while the gross expenditure was £3,445,773 — a net loss of £1,171,569.

The following year, ending 30 June 1923, the fleet earned £2,529,800 with an expenditure amounting to £4,155,959 — a net loss of £1,626,159. The effect of ballast voyages showed up in the Balance Sheet. The newly appointed Shipping Board had the unenviable task of transforming these losses into profits. The 54 ships in the 1923 listing were a considerable fleet, and many of them had been laid up for months. Even before the 1923 Act came into operation, the sale of some of these ships was being negotiated and, within a few weeks of the Board's formation, 25 ships were sold, 9 of these to Japanese buyers. The book value of the fleet had been drastically reduced prior to the sale.

The position in connection with the disposal of surplus tonnage during the period 1 September 1923 to 31 March 1925 was as follows:-

Capital value for 26 steamers sold	£610,150.0.0.
Sale Price (Less Commissions etc.)	£648,180.0.0.
Excess of sale price over book value	£ 38,030.0.0.
Expenses of lay up, including interest and sale charges on vessels sold	£ 52,233.12.8
Expenses of lay up, including interest and depreciation on 17 vessels awaiting sale at 31st March, 1925	£ 90,014.2.2
Total	£142,247.14.10
Excess on sales as above	£ 38,030.0.0.
Deficiency	£104,217.14.10

This statement shows that out of the 50 ships and the four under construction at the time of the Shipping Board's first meeting, 26 had been sold and 17 were listed for sale, leaving a fleet of 11 ships. By the end of 1925 the sale of the 17 ships had been finalised and four others were laid up awaiting buyers, leaving a fleet of seven, the five Bay ships and the two Dales. In spite of this drastic pruning, the Australian Commonwealth Line of Steamers showed a loss on operations for the year 1925-1926 of £503,077.

The year 1926 showed a further decline. The Balance Sheet produced on 31 March 1926 showed liabilities of £6,387,624 and assets £5,058,790. The Parliamentary Joint Committee of Public Accounts was instructed to investigate a report on the activities of the Line. As migration was now one of the main sources of earnings of the Australian Commonwealth Line, a brief commentary of this facet of Government Policy would not be amiss. Britain was the main recruitment area for would-be migrants to Australia, mainly the industrial areas where, in 1926, unemployment had reached a figure representing 7%. The British "Dole" as it was always referred to, was really unemployment insurance. During the period of employment, weekly wage deductions were made; whilst unemployed a payment of 18/- per week was made to single men, married men getting further allowances for dependants. These payments or "Dole" were only paid in proportion to the number of tax stamps on the insurance card.

Around the walls of the employment office, usually a condemned school building pressed into service to cope with the increasing number of applicants, were posters extolling the delights of work on the land in Australia. Each State had its own scheme, though Tasmania and South Australia did not advertise. Western Australia had a poster in which a bronzed character beckoned from a field of golden wheat to come to join him. Victoria used apple orchards as a similar lure; New South Wales oranges, and Queensland, sugar cane. They all aimed to attract the 18 years old section. Victoria had the "Big Brothers Scheme", New South Wales the "Dreadnought Scheme", and Queensland the "Farm Apprentice Scheme". Other age groups could only be nominated privately. At this time Australia also had a growing army of unemployed in the main cities and could not guarantee any employment other than that on the land, where the

Industrial Courts had no Awards regarding pay and conditions. This year, 1926, was a black one in Britain's history — a six months strike by coal miners, not for increased pay, but against a solid reduction in pay, culminating in the general strike, perhaps the closest Britain has been to Civil War since Oliver Cromwell's days. Those who could raise the £11 necessary to migrate to Australia did so. £2 landing money was also required. This was returned to the migrant on disembarkation. The poster displaying blue skies and sunshine had their effect. There was plenty of time to study them as they stood apprehensively in the Dole queues not knowing whether they would get cash, or a notice that benefits had ceased. For each voyage of the Bay Ships to Australia accommodation was fully booked. There was no shortage of the 18 year class. These lads had left school at 14, experiencing little difficulty in securing employment. At the age of 18, when higher wages were required, they became redundant and were replaced by other 14 year old school leavers.

There was no welcome mat out for the migrants as they disembarked at the Australian ports. The city dwellers who had jobs could only see the new arrivals as a threat. From 1925 onwards pressure was put on the Government to stop the flow but, as the Commonwealth Government of that time represented rural interests who depended on migrant labour, nothing was done to halt the granting of assisted passages. The expression "adjectival Pommy" had a great deal of invective used with it. Queensland's farm apprentice scheme involved the signing of a three year indenture to be taught farming. Pay for the first 3 months at 15s. 0d. per week, 17s 6d. for the remainder of the year. The second year apprentice was paid £1, the third year 25s. 0d. per week. The farmer only paid a small portion directly. The remainder was paid into the local Clerk of Petty Sessions for remission to the State Migration Office in Brisbane to be credited to the Bank account of the apprentice, who would be entitled to draw on this on attaining the age of 21. The theory was that he would then buy a farm of his own, but some celebrated their 21st birthday with a visit to the office of the Australian Commonwealth Line and booking a passage home. Others married farmers' daughters and settled down to live happily ever after.

Chapter 13.

EPILOGUE

The year 1926 was also one of record drought in the Eastern States of Australia. Districts with an average rainfall of 40 inches had rain in mid-January and no more for eleven months. The Bay Ships each had a cargo capacity of 900,000 cubic feet of which 370,000 cubic feet were insulated. Much of this insulated space was filled in Brisbane, butter, cheese and meat being Queensland's main exports. Consequently the cargoes carried on the ships of the Commonwealth Line were well below capacity, though the year was a record one for assisted British Migrants — a total of 31,260 compared with the 24,827 who arrived in 1925. Industrial trouble mounted amongst the various maritime unions. The Waterside Workers' Federation, who supplied all the labour used on the Australian Wharves, kept their books closed to ensure full employment for their

36 "CERAMIC"

Built 1913, 18,000 tons. Owned by White Star Line, later merged into Shaw Savill and Albion Line. This was the largest ship on the London–Australia via Cape route and held that distinction for many years. Lost by enemy action in South Atlantic during the early years of World War 2. All "Cabin" Class. From 1930 sailed as unit of White Star–Aberdeen–Blue Funnel Joint Service.

37 "PERICLES"

10,925 tons, built in 1908 in Belfast for Aberdeen Line. In common with other ships of this line, she had accommodation for 100 first class passengers and 400 third class. On 31st March, 1910 whilst on voyage to London struck an uncharted rock, and sank in 16 fathoms of water just over seven miles off Cape Leeuwin lighthouse, Western Australia. Boats were lowered and within half an hour the entire complement of 463 crew and passengers were safely disembarked, *Pericles* sinking shortly afterwards. Amongst the cargo were several hundred tons of lead ingots. In 1957 much of this was salvaged, and resumed its interrupted voyage to the London market.

"NESTOR"

Alfred Hot & Co. Blue Funnell Line, 14,500 tons.

"ULYSSES"

Commissioned in 1913. Sister ship to *Nestor*. Both these vessels built for Australian—Passenger—Cargo Trade. Each had accommodation for 255 one class passengers. They were active as troop carriers during the two World Wars. Apart from war service, *Nestor* made 68 voyages U.K.—Brisbane via Cape and steamed 2,100,000 miles before being scrapped after going out of commission July 27, 1950. *Ulysses* was torpedoed and sunk by U.160 off the coast of Florida in 1942. Speed of these ships was 14 knots on a coal consumption of 140 tons per day.

"VICTORIA"

P & O Line. One of four sister ships known as the "Jubilee Ships". Commissioned in 1887, the year of Queen Victoria's Jubilee. The other three ships were *Brittania*, *Arcadia* and *Oceana*. They were built to maintain the Australian mail services and the ever increasing migration from Europe to Australia. With accommodation for 410 passengers and cargo capacity of 4,000 tons, they provided comfort and speed, thus making migration more attractive. Their speed of 16 knots on a coal consumption of 110 tons of coal per day made these vessels profitable to the P & O Company.

members; on the rare occasions the books had been opened preference was always given to members' sons, following the tradition of the Thames Watermen. There was also a strike of ships' stewards; shipowners threatened to put on "Free Labour" of which there was a plentiful supply. 1927 was another good year for migrants when 30,123 assisted migrants arrived. One third of these were single girls, nominated by the Migration Offices of the various States. There was a strong demand for domestic servants. Most middle class homes kept a maid, whose wage varied between 10/- and £1 per week, according to age and experience. The migrant girls had little difficulty in finding such work, but their lot was not an enviable one. Dr Barnardo's Homes in Britain co-operated with the Commonwealth Government in this regard. For each migrant accepted by the States, the Commonwealth made £75 available in loan funds at a low rate of interest. Travellers arriving at Sydney by sea are always impressed by the peace and tranquility of Sydney Harbour; unfortunately this idyllic scene stopped at the shore. In the years of industrial unrest during the late 1920's in the streets of Woolloomooloo and around the Argyle Cut and along the Sussex Street Wharves, the scenes were far from peaceful. The unemployment rate was close to 10%, men were torn between loyalties to their Unions or to their families. Through this, the ships of the Australian Commonwealth Line managed to keep sailing, not always on schedule, and sometimes leaving cargoes behind.

The year 1927 finished in an atmosphere of explosive tension. On Tuesday, 27 December, the stewards of the *Moreton Bay* staged another walk off, leaving Australia's dignitaries lunchless. Moreton Bay was anchored in Sydney Harbour acting as a Regatta Flagship. The remainder of the ship's crew could not reach a decision. Some supported the action of the stewards, others condemned it. The factions had the ship in a turmoil. Disciplinary action was taken by the Ship's Captain. This brought out the stewards on all the Australian Ships. They remained on strike until 11 January 1928, and then returned on the shipowners' terms. The *Moreton Bay* had missed her sailing, so the entire crew were paid off and the ship laid up until her next sailing date of 20 March.

The Marine Cooks and Bakers Union embarked on another prolonged strike. This one lasted 15 weeks. They went back on the owners' terms on 21 June 1928. Cooks as a class are as temperamental as Prima Donnas, and the seagoing section have much to put up with. As a member of that fraternity I can speak with much feeling on their trials and tribulations. However Judge Dethbridge of the Commonwealth Arbitration Court gave little sympathy to the Marine Cooks and Bakers and cancelled their award, the effect being no rights or benefits under the award would accrue to the Union or any employee, nor would any obligation be incurred by shipowners. Lighthouse keepers around Australia's Coasts had been living on emergency rations as the Union-managed Lighthouse Supply Ships failed to make their regular calls. The Commonwealth Government issued a Gazette placing the crews of Lighthouse Supply Ships under the Commonwealth Public Service, thus entirely eliminating the influence of the Maritime Unions. Applications were called, with an overwhelming response and the Lighthouse Ships sailed on their essential voyages. They have been manned by Public Service employees ever since.

King Coal reigned supreme in Australia making the Miners' Union all powerful. Strikes had been successful, but had sent up the price of coal. Best Northumberland coal shipped from Newcastle-on-Tyne could be landed on the

Newcastle, New South Wales Wharves at 7s. 0d. per ton less than the local product. The South Australian Government, for many years a large buyer of New South Wales coal, gave their coal orders to English collieries at 35s. 6d. per ton landed at Adelaide, 10s. 0d. less than landed New South Wales supplies. Some imported bunkering coal was landed at Launceston, Tasmania. The Bass Straits passenger and cargo liner *Loongana* called into the Launceston Coal Wharf to replenish her bunkers for the return voyage to Melbourne. The Waterside Workers' Federation had declared it "black", so *Loongana* had to sail without it. It had been calculated that supplies of coal already on board would get the ship back to Melbourne. After a particularly rough passage which increased the coal consumption beyond expectation, *Loongana* arrived off Port Philip Bay with empty bunkers and no steam. Only the arrival of three Melbourne tugs prevented what could have been a disastrous shipwreck.

It was in this atmosphere of industrial chaos that the fate of the Australian Commonwealth Line of steamers was decided. No time was wasted once the decision to sell had been made. Tenders closed on 28 January, only a month after the stewards of the *Moreton Bay* had refused to serve lunch to the Governor-General. The sale of the line was to be finalised in April. One clause in the tender compelled the buyers to maintain a service equal to that of the Commonwealth Shipping Board and to maintain an efficient Australian organisation. The Waterside Workers' Federation of Australia, Painters and Dockers Union and other Maritime Unions had already announced that the ships would be declared black if ever they returned to Australia. In those circumstances, it is not surprising that only three tenders were submitted — none of them generous. That of the White Star Line for £1,900,000 was accepted. The deal involved the five "Bay" Ships and the two "Dale" Ships, 100 A.1 at Lloyds, aggregating a net tonnage of 53,420 tons.

Other maritime news for the early part of 1928 were *Ferndale* arriving at Melbourne with two of the largest packing cases ever to arrive in Australia. Each case was valued at £17,000 and contained the components for two super-marine Southampton Flying Boats. The B.H.P. Steamer *Iron Chief* ex *Mandy Lodge* ex *Elmtree* went aground at Mermaid Reef, near Diamond Head on 1 April 1928. *Iron Chief* and her cargo of 11,227 railway sleepers were sold two weeks later for £550. In South Australia the Adelaide Steamship Company manned their s.s. *Paringa* with office staff to take supplies to Port Lincoln. In Queensland, the Brisbane shipowner, John Burke, whose ships had always been painted green, changed the hull colour to black, remarking that his ships had been declared "black" so often they might as well remain that way. The Australian Commonwealth Line declared a loss of £584,377 for the year 1927-28 and the flag of H.M.A.S. *Sydney* was hauled down at noon on Tuesday 8 May 1928. From that time, the famous cruiser which had destroyed the elusive *Emden* on 9 November 1914, ceased to be a unit of The Royal Australian Navy. Her mast on Bradleys Head is a permanent memorial to one of Australia's fighting ships.

There was to be no reprieve for the Australian Commonwealth Line; as each vessel arrived in Port, arrangements were made for the ships to be delivered to London. Those members of the crews who desired to be repatriated back to Australia were given tickets to travel as passengers. The last ship to leave Australia flying the flag of the Commonwealth Line was *Ferndale*. She departed from

Sydney on 19 June 1928. After a heated debate in the House of Representatives there was no opposition to the disposal of the line. The general public were completely indifferent. No scathing "Letters to the Editor" appeared in any of the newspapers. The general atmosphere of 1928 was one of fear of the future and disappointment with the past. The hopes of the brave new world which was to rise from wreckage of war had failed to materialise and the spirit of nationalism which had built up the Commonwealth Line had evaporated. In Queensland numerous other such ventures, State fisheries, State canneries, State butchers shops, farms and produce agents had closed down with heavy losses to the taxpayers. If the average Australian displayed any feeling at all about the demise of the shipping venture, it was one of relief.

The Waterside Workers Federation were in no position to enforce a black ban against the ships, sailing under the flag of the White Star Line. Volunteer labour was engaged for wharf work, after an ultimatum had expired ordering the Federation to resume work. A cancellation of the award followed. An uneasy peace was eventually declared, the Federal Government insisting that the free labour already working on the wharf be admitted to the Waterside Workers Federation. It was obvious that this would cause much acrimony along the waterfront of Australia's Ports. The "free labour" section were known as "28" men. An endeavour was made to keep them in separate gangs for the sake of harmony, but the feelings of bitterness amongst the old hands in the Federation were too deep to forgive and forget. The "28" men lived a pariah-like existence on the wharves. Many broke under the strain and left the industry. Others carried on regardless, though they were never accepted and for decades afterwards the term "28 men" was used as an expression of contempt. The "Bays" and the "Dales" continued on the U.K. — Australia run, and no black ban was ever imposed. The 1929 Lloyds Shipping Register showed only the Lighthouse Supply Ships under the ownership of the Australian Government, as in 1916 when T.S.S. *Merimbula* was the sole listing, before being joined by the "Australs" and the three score other ships which flew the flag of the Australian Government.

As the story of the Australian Shipping venture started with T.S.S. *Merimbula* perhaps it is fitting that her life finished one week before the sale of the line was finalised. On 27 March 1928 *Merimbula* ran aground off Beecroft Head, 100 miles south of Sydney, N.S.W. A few days later she was sold by auction for the sum of £300. At the time *Merimbula* was serving in the fleet of the Illawarra and South Coast Steamship Co., better known as "The Pig and Whistle Line", the reason for this designation being that the ships served farmers on the river systems of Southern New South Wales. Apart from produce carried below deck, pigs were carried as deck cargo. It was the practice of the Captains of this Company's ship to sound the ship's steam whistle when some miles from the landing to give the farmers chance to muster their pigs and get them down to the wharf ready for loading. The headquarters of the Illawarra and South Coast S.S. Co. were at the Sussex Street Wharves in Sydney — once the heart of Sydney's coastal shipping trade.

Unlike the countries of the old world whose histories seem to consist of Royal intrigues, histories in which the ordinary type of man seemed to have no place, Australia's history is a most colourful one. That of the explorers has been well documented, that of the pioneers less so, doubtless they were too busy by day and too tired at night to record their work for posterity. Coastal and Overseas

Shipping history has been sadly neglected. The well known Australian coastal shipping companies retain their names but have no ships. They have diversified their activities into other fields of investment. Their proud history of service as pioneer Australians has been largely forgotten. Some are wharfingers, tourist bureaus, tug owners and ship repairers. The younger generation working in their offices know nothing about the ships that made the names of these firms famous throughout the world. Having seen some of the ships of the Commonwealth Line, worked with those who manned them, and above all having a strong affection for ships and the sea, I trust this compilation will be of benefit to Australia and Australians. To William Morris Hughes and those who supported him in bringing his vision to fulfilment, the words of Omar Khayyam may seem appropriate — "The worldly hope men set their hearts upon — turns ashes — or it prospers and anon, like snow upon the desert dusty face, Lighting a little hour or two — is gone".

Fare structures, August 1936:

Aberdeen and Commonwealth Line:

Southampton to Brisbane, 6 berth cabin C deck, Single £39, return £58.10.0.

White Star — Aberdeen Joint Service 3rd class:

Liverpool-Brisbane *Themistocles.* Single £36, return £54.

Ceramic Cabin class Single £67, return £117
Special rate return within eight months £100.10.0.

Blue Funnel, Alfred Holt and Co. First class only, *Nestor* and *Ulysses.*

Liverpool-Brisbane Single £72, return £126. Special rate return £114.

APPENDIX "A"
THE COMMONWEALTH FLEET ON 31ST JULY, 1923
(Commonwealth Shipping Act 1923 – The Schedule)

Line	Steamer	Built	Gross Tonnage	Total Tonnage
"Austral" (11 vessels)	Australbrook	1909	4,336	
	Australcrag	1907	4,503	
	Australford	1907	4,403	
	Australglen	1906	4,417	
	Australmead	1912	4,151	
	Australmount	1909	4,338	
	Australpeak	1906	4,432	
	Australplain	1907	4,454	
	Australpool	1906	4,326	
	Australport	1915	3,570	
	Australrange	1907	4,409	47,339
"Ex-enemy" (17 vessels)	Araluen	1901	5,519	
	Bakara	1913	5,970	
	Barambah	1912	6,016	
	Boonah	1912	6,011	
	Booral	1905	4,359	
	Boorara	1913	6,570	
	Bulga	1903	1,449	
	Bulla	1905	5,099	
	Culula	1907	4,265	
	Carina	1907	5,486	
	Cooee	1907	4,255	
	Dongarra	1906	5,601	
	Gilgai	1901	5,512	
	Parattah	1904	4,229	
	Talawa	1907	3,834	
	Toromeo	1905	4,149	
	Mawatta	1904	1,096	79,420
"D" (6 vessels)	Delungra	1919–20	3,346	
	Dilga	1919–20	3,308	
	Dinoga	1919–20	3,341	
	Dromana	1919–20	3,350	
	Dumosa	1919–20	3,351	
	Dundula	1919–20	3,344	20,040

Line	Steamer	Built	Gross Tonnage	Total Tonnage
"E" (13 vessels)	Emita	1921–2	3,347	
	Enoggera	1921–2	3,359	
	Eurelia	1921–2	3,351	
	Eromanga	1921–2	3,359	
	Echuca	1921–2	3,362	
	Echunga	1921–2	3,362	
	Erriba	1921–2	3,345	
	Eudunda	1921–2	3,352	
	Eugowra	1921–2	3,344	
	Euwarra	1921–2	3,349	
	Eurimbla	1921–2	3,351	
	Elouera	1923–4	3,353	
	Euroa	1923–4	3,353	43,587
"Dale" (2 vessels)	Fordsdale	1923	9,700	
	Ferndale	1924	9,700	19,400
"Bay" (5 vessels)	Moreton Bay	1921	13,850	
	Hobson's Bay	1921	13,837	
	Jervis Bay	1922	13,837	
	Largs Bay	1922	13,851	
	Esperance Bay	1922	13,851	69,226
54 vessels				279,012

VESSELS TORPEDOED, WRECKED, OR SOLD PRIOR TO 30th JUNE, 1923
(Accounted for in S.M. Bruce's first financial statement)

Australbush (torpedoed)	Cardinia
Australdale	Barunga
Australfield	Carawa (wrecked)
Australstream	Conargo
John Murray (wrecked)	Canowie
Shandon	Burrowa
Speedway	Cooroy
Samoa	Carrabin

APPENDIX "B"
BRUCE'S FIRST FINANCIAL STATEMENT
Showing Position of Commonwealth Fleet at 30th June, 1923

Capital Expenditure and Losses			Profits, Recoveries and Present Market Values	
Capital cost of Vessels in Commission (detailed in original		£11,818,938	Gross Profit on Commonwealth Line	£ 2,493,449
			Insurance Reserve	901,920
Estimated cost of Vessels in course of Construction (detailed in original)		2,338,000	Proceeds from Sale of Vessels (detailed in original)	299,433
Capital cost of Vessels lost and/or sold (detailed in original)		807,808	Amounts recovered on account of vessels lost at sea (detailed in original)	791,897
Interest paid and payable to 30.6.23 by the Line to the Commonwealth Bank and Treasury on overdraft	£684,876		Interest received from Underwriters on account of vessels lost and sold	1,738
Less Interest charged on account of detained enemy vessels, debited the Line Account current but for which the Treasury did not pay	127,512	557,364	Profit on Ex-enemy vessels prior to incorporation in fleet	3,673,494
			Present day market value of vessels in commission and in course of construction	4,718,150
Furniture & Fittings at cost		11,232	Book value of office furniture & fittings	7,500
Stores in Hand		23,700	Estimated value of stores on hand 30.6.23	23,700
			Balance — being estimated total debit on all transactions	2,645,761
		£15,557,042		£15,557,042

Hansard Volume 103 p. 645.

APPENDIX "C"
BRUCE'S SECOND FINANCIAL STATEMENT
Showing Position of Commonwealth Fleet at 31st March, 1928

LIABILITIES —

Treasury Debentures			£4,725,650
Treasury for Interest			1,054,600
			£5,780,250

ASSETS —

Book Value of Fleet		£2,747,000	
Furniture and Fittings		6,500	
Spare Gear		40,000	
		£2,793,500	
Investments	£303,400		
Less Overdraft	120,000		
		183,400	
			2,976,900
Shrinkage of Assets			2,803,350

MADE UP BY —

Voyage Losses		497,450	
Administration Expenses, less Commission, Brokerage, Interest, etc.		310,750	
Depreciation		703,450	
Debenture Interest		985,550	
		£2,497,200	
Loss on sale of Surplus Tonnage		536,200	
			3,033,400
Less Insurance Reserve Account		110,000	
Bunkers, Provisions and Stores Reserve Account		113,000	223,000
			£2,790,400

Difference represents balances at 31st March between Sundry Creditors and Sundry Debtors
    Debit Balances and Credit Balances on pending voyages and on closed voyages
    Agents' Credit Balances and Debit Balances.

Balances not yet recovered on
    Average Accounts, Cargo Claims, Medical Claims, etc.

These cannot be determined until accounts to 31st March, from London and Branch offices are received.

Hansard Vol. 118 p. 4340.

INDEX

Prepared by Mavis Michell
See also separate Index of Ships

A

A.U.S.N., 12, 45-47, 51-2.
Aberdeen and Commonwealth line, 9, 15-17.
Aberdeen Line, 13, 15, 26.
Acts. *See* Australia. Laws, statutes, etc.
Adelaide Steamship Co, 12, 58.
Asquith, Herbert, Prime Minister of Great Britain, 4-5.
Austral ships, 6, 12, 18-29, 30.
Australasian United Steam Navigation. *See* A.U.S.N.
Australia. Laws, statutes, etc. Acts Navigation Act, 1912, 6, 13; Shipping Act 1923 30, 54;
Australian Government Line of Steamers. *See under earlier name,* Commonwealth Government Shipping Line.
Australian War Memorial, 46.
Australian Wheat Board, 22, 25.
Austrian Lloyd Co., 28.

B

Ballast voyages, 22-23, 54.
Barclay, Curle & Co., Glasgow, shipbuilders, 9, 25.
Barquentines, 8.
Bay ships, 10, 12-17, 48-50, 56, 59.
Beardsmore Wm. & Co., Clyde shipbuilders, 48.
Black Germans, ships, 4.
Black pan watch, 36.
Boilers, care of, 32.
Bottle message from *Mareeba* crew, 46.
Bremen-Vulcan, Vegesack, 27-28, 32.
Broken Hill Co. Pty. Ltd., 9, 13, 23, 45-47.
Bruce, S.M., Prime Minister of Australia, 4, 13-15; quoted on American built ships, 42.
Brunel, Isambard, 53.
Burns, Philp & Co., 10, 13.
Burrell & Sons, Glasgow, 6, 18, 21.

C

Caddy, H.O., Lt.-Col., 11.
Cambay Prince Steamship Co., 43.
Canadian tramp steamers, 26.
Captain, name coupled with ship in advertising, 16.
Cargo carrying shipping lines, 9-10.
Cargoes, difficulty in obtaining, 25, 44.
Cargoes of Austral ships, 18-24; of American built ships, 42. *See also* Case oil cargoes; coal cargoes; sugar cargoes; wheat cargoes.
Carpsey Steamship Co., 23.
Case oil cargo, 23.
Chief engineers, 36.
Coal, bunker, 19-20.
Coal burning ships, 19-20, 25, 34-39; arduous work on, 34.
Coal cargoes, 57-58.
Coastal passenger services, 13, 51-52.
Coastal shipping companies, 12, 34.
Coastal trade, 2, 12; of American built ships, 42; of D class ships, 43; of E class ships, 44-47; in Western Australia 31.
Cockatoo Dock, Sydney, 6, 9-10.
Commonwealth and Dominion Line, 9.
Commonwealth Government Shipping Line: competition with other lines, 9, 12, 14, 34; purchase prices, 14, 47; establishment of, 8, 25, 27; expansion of fleet, 6-8, 41; and reduction, 12, 50, industrial troubles, 2, 14, 26, 30, 57-58; maintenance of ships, 32-33; migration services, 8, 49, 55; profits and losses, 14, 18, 32-33, 44, 54-55, 58-59, Appx. B (for financial statements); reorganization, 54, routes, 10, sale, 14-16, 54-55, 58-59; *See also* Hughes, William Morris; *and names of ships and classes of ships.*
Cook, Sir Joseph, Leader of the Opposition, 5-6.
Cooks, Bakers and Butchers Association (Marine), 14, 57.
Craggs, R. & Sons, Middleborough, shipbuilders, 28.
Crews wages and conditions: on Australian ships, 13, 34; on British ships, 33-35, 37-38; on coal-burning ships, 30, 34-35.
Cunard Line, 33.

D

D class ships, 6-7, 12, 42-43, 47.
Dale ships, 9-10, 12, 15, 53, 59.
Defence potential of Bay and Dale ships, 14.
Delays in shipping, 26-27.
Denny, Wm. and Brothers, Dumbarton, shipbuilders, 51.
The Depression, 1929; effect on shipping, 16.
Deutsche Australische Co., 10.
Distressed British seamen, 50.
Drought, 1926: effect on shipping, 56.
Dry dock method of shipbuilding, 53.
Ducal Shipping Line, 3-4.
Duncan & Co., Glasgow, shipbuilders, 18-21.
Dutch East Indies, Trade with, 43.

E

E class ships, 12, 44-47.
Ellerman Bucknall, 10.
Em-Hadjillas, 32-33.
Erikson, Captain, 26.

F

Federal Steam Navigation Co., 9.
Ferguson, Sir Ronald (Gov.-Gen.), 11.
Fares, coastal passenger, 13, 51.
Farm Apprentice Scheme, Queensland, 55-56.
Fires in ex-German ships, 30.
Fisher, Andrew, Prime Minister, 4-5.
Free labour on wharves, 59.
Freight rates 9; coastal, 47, decline in, 10, 23; made level with overseas companies, 14.
Furness, Withy & Co., West Hartlepool, shipbuilders, 9, 25.

G

German ships (interned during 1st World War, 4, 6, 8, 27-34.
Gilroy, Norman, Cardinal, 4.
Grangemount and Greenock Dockyard, Clyde, 22-24.
Gt. Britain Board of Trade: agreement with crews, 37; conditions on ships, 33-34.

H

Hamburg-South American Line, 28.
Hamilton Shipbuilding Co., Glasgow, 19, 22.
Harland and Wolff's Shipyard, 17.
Helsingfors Co., Helsinki, 28.
Henderson. H. & W., Glasgow, shipbuilders, 24.
Horse transports in 1st World War, 33.
Howard Smith, 12.
Huddard Parker, 43, 49.
Hughes, W.M., Prime Minister: early life in England, 2; Billy Hughes' ships, 2; migration to and early experiences in Australia, 3; political and union activity, 3; at Imperial Conference, 3; became Prime Minister, 4; initial purchase of ships, 5-6; arranged building of coastal ships, 6; purchase of American ships, 6; resignation and re-appointment as Prime Minister, 8-10; at Peace Conference, 1919, 8; return journey, 11-12; resignation as Prime Minister, 12; opposed sale of Commonwealth Government Shipping Line, 13-15; death, 18.
Hughes, Martin & Washington, Sydney, shipbuilders, 39.

I

Illawarra and South Coast Steamship Co., 59.
Industrial unrest in maritime industries, 14, 30, 56-57.
Influenza epidemic: Effect on shipping, 27, 30.

J

James Patrick & Co., Melbourne, 31.
James Paterson & Co., Melbourne, 43.
Japanese shipping companies, 9.

K

Kidman & Mayoh, Sydney, shipbuilders, 8, 39.
Kneen, G.H., 54.
Kylsant, Lord, 16.
Kylsant Group, 15-16.

L

Labour troubles in maritime industries, 14, 30, 56-57.
Larkin, H.B.G., 5, 54.
Launching of ships, 53.
Lifeboat stowage and launching, 52.
Lighthouse supply ships, 57, 59.
Lloyd George, David, Prime Minister, 6.
Lloyds Shipping Register, 2, 6, 8, 27, 32-33, 59.

M

McIlwraith, McEacharn, 45.
McMillan, A., Dumbarton, shipbuilder, 24.
Manners Steamship Co., Hong Kong, 45.
Marine Cooks and Bakers Union, (Marine Cooks, Bakers and Butchers Association), 57.
Maritime unions: achieved good working conditions, 34; objected to passage workers, 49; involved in labour troubles, 56-57.
Matzuaka Kizen, 22.
Merchant Officers Guild, 30.
Migrant girls for domestic service, 57.
Migrants, schemes for, 55-56.
Migration: after 1st World War, 8, 16; shipping lines used for, 13; after 2nd World War, 17, 49-50, 55-56; staffing of ships for, 49-50.

N

Napier and Miller, Glasgow, shipbuilders, 9, 19, 25.
National Seamen's and Firemen's Union (Gt. Britain), 14, 35.
Navigation Act, 1912, 6, 13.
Naval Dockyard, Sydney, 8, 44.
Naval officers, staffing of merchant ships by, 1-2.
New Settlers' League, 23.
New Zealand Shipping Co., 9.
Newcastle, N.S.W. Government Shipyards, 6, 8, 44.
Nosgood, S.A., 54.
Norddeutscher Lloyd, 28, 30.

O

Oil burning ships, 31.
Onassis, Aristotle, 26.

P

P. & O. Line, 13, 16.
Pacific S.N. Co., 15.
Panamanian Oriental Steamship Co., 27.
Passage workers on migrant ships, 49-50.
Passenger ships, 13, 16, 49-50. *See also* Coastal passenger services.
Patterson, McDonald Shipbuklding Co., 41.
Pig and Whistle Line, 59.
Poland Line, Bremen, 28.
Poole & Steele, Adelaide, shipbuilders, 7, 8.
Port Line. *See* Commonwealth and Dominion Line.
Pound and pint conditions of British Board of Trade, 33, 34.
Public rooms on ocean liners, 51.

Q

Queensland Farm Apprentice Scheme, 55-56.

R

Railway development, effect on shipping, 12, 49, 52.
Recruitment of crews in Britain, 35, 37.
Refrigerated shipping, 10, 28, 30, 32-33.
Rockhampton, Port of, 25, 45.
Rodger & Co., Glasgow, 8, 40.
Royal Mail Co., 15.
Russian scare, 3.

S

Sailing ships of the Commonwealth Government Shipping Line, 39-40.
Sailing ships, Finnish, 26.
Seamen, Australian, working conditions of, 1, 9.
Seamen, British; wages, 15; working conditions, 9; unemployment, 16.
Seamen's Union, 2, 14, 30.
Scottish Shire Lines, 9.
Shaw, Savill & Co., 15-16.
Sheepskin coats for troops, 33.
Shipbuilding, Australian: contracts, 39; high quality of, 45.
Shipping Act, 1923, 30, 54.
Shipping lack for Australian produce, 1915, 4-5.
Shipping losses in 1st World War, 4, 6-7, 41.
Shipping slump, 8-9, 15-16.
Skinner, Captain of *Mareeba*, 46.
Sloan Shipyard, Seattle, 7, 41.
South Australian ports: lack of loading facilities, 26.
Stewards' Union, (Federated Marine Stewards and Pantrymen's Association of Australia), 14, 57.
Stewart, Wm. & Co., 23.
Stokers and stoking, 35-36.
Stonehaven, John Lawrence, Baron (Gov.-Gen.), 14.
Stowaways on *Jervis Bay*, 15.
Strath ships, 6, 18-24.
Strathairly Steamship Co., 21.
Strikes by maritime unions, 57.
Sugar cargoes from Cuba, 22, 24.
Swan Wigham, Newcastle-on-Tyne, shipbuilders, 31.
Sydney Harbour. Regatta, 1927, 14, 57.

T

Thierault, A., Nova Scotia, shipbuilders, 40.
Thompson & Co., Castlemaine, Vic., shipbuilders, 42.
The Times, London: quoted on Lord Kylsant, 16; on sale of Commonwealth Government Shipping Line, 15.
Torpedoed Australian ships: *Australbush*, 19; *Kyarra*, 52; *Mareeba*, 46.
Townsville, in 2nd World War, 40.
Troop and horse transports, 1st World War, 28, 30, 33, 40.
"28" men, 59.

U

Unemployment in Britain, 16, 55-56.
Unions, 14, 30, 34, 35, 49, 56, 57, 58, 59.

V

Vickers, Barrow in Furness, shipbuilders, 10, 48.

W

Walkers Ltd., Maryborough, Qld., shipbuilders, 7-9, 44.
Wallace Power Boat Co., Sydney, 39.
Waterfront labour, casual system, 34.
Waterside Workers' Federation, 56, 58-59.
Western Australian Shipbuilding Co., 39.
Western Australian coastal shipping services, 31.
Wheat cargoes, 19, 28, 32; as German famine relief, 22; bulk handling of, 25-26; on passenger ships, 25; on sailing ships, 26.
White Star Line, 15, 25-26, 58-59.
Williamstown, Victoria. Commonwealth Ship Construction Branch, 6, 42, 44.
Wooden ships, American built, 8-9.
World War, 1914-1918, 4, 52.
World War, 1939-1945, ships commandeered for use in, 17.
Wrecked ships: *Carawa*, 28-29; *Ferndale*, 15, 45; *John Murray*, 39-40; *Kanowna*, 52; *Koombana*, 31; *Milora*, 45.

THE COMMONWEALTH SHIPPING LINE
INDEX TO SHIPS

A

Adonis, 3.
Adriatic, 25.
Akaroa ex *Euripedes*, 16.
Akuna I ex *Una*, 27.
Akuna II ex *Gladstone*, 27.
Albertina ex *Rosanna* became *Kotka*, 28.
Altona became *Conargo*, 29.
Aorangi, 3.
Araluen ex *Scharzfels*, 33.
Arawa ex *Esperance Bay I*, 16-17.
Ardangorm, became *Australport*, 9, 25.
Ardanmhor became *Australplain*, 24.
Asaka Maru ex *Australmount*, 22.
Australbrook ex *Strathesk* became *Uga Maru*, 9, 18-19.
Australbush ex *Strathgarry*, 19.
Australcrag ex *Strathleven* became *Misaka Maru*, 20.
Australdale ex *Strathendrick*, 19.
Australfield ex *Vermont*, became *Liberta*, became *Dimitrios N. Rallas*, 9, 17, 25.
Australford ex *Strathavon* became *Unyo Maru*, 23-24.
Australglen ex *Strathord* became *Ginro Maru*, 24.
Australia, H.M.A.S., 50.
Australmount ex *Strathbeg* became *Asaka Maru*, 22.
Australmead ex *Kirkoswald*, 24.
Australpeak ex *Strathspey* became *Carpsey*, 22-23.
Australplain ex *Ardanmhor*, 9, 24-25.
Australpool ex *Strathairly* became *Miho Maru*, 18, 21-22.
Australport ex *Ardangorm*, 9, 25.
Australrange ex *Strathdee* became *Ishikari Maru*, 20-21.
Australstream ex *Dalton Hall*, became *General Degoute*, 9, 25.

B

Babinda, 8, 41.
Bakara ex *Cannstatt* became *Witell, Rosario, Albertina, Kotka*, 10, 28.
Balcatta, 41.
Baltic, 3, 25.
Bambra ex *Prinz Sigmund*, 10, 31.
Barambah ex *Hobart*, 33.
Barungra ex *Sumatra*, 33.
Bellata, 8, 10, 41-42.
Benowa, 8, 41.
Berlin became *Parattah*, 6, 32.
Berringa, 8, 10, 41.
Bethanga, 8, 10, 41-42.
Biloela, 2.
Birriwa, 8, 10, 41.
Blackwater, 9,
Boko, 3.
Boobyalla, 41.
Boonah ex *Melbourne* became *Witram*, 30.
Booral ex *Oberhausen* became *Atlas*, 12, 27, 33.
Boorara ex *Pfalz* became *Nereus*, 12, 27, 32, 33.
Borrika, 41.
Braeside, 8, 39, 40.
Bulga, 31.
Bulla, ex *Hessen* became *Weissessee*, 12, 27, 29.
Bundarra, 8, 10, 41.
Burnside, 8, 39-40.

C

Calcutta ex *Osnabruck*, 33.
Canadian Fisher, 26.
Canadian Trooper, 26.
Cannstatt became *Bakara*, 10.
Cape Leeuwin, 2.
Cape York, 2.
Captain Rokos ex *Carina*, 28.
Cardinia ex *Olinda*, 8, 40.
Carina, ex *Griefswald* became *Captain Rokos*, 12, 27-28.
Carpsey ex *Australpeak*, 23.
Cedric, 25.
Celtic, 25.
Ceramic, 26.
Cerberus, H.M.A.S., 21.
Cethana, 8, 41.
Challamba, 7, 41.
Clyde Breeze, ex *Easby*, 43.
Colac ex *Dinoga* became *Easby*, 43.
Conargo ex *Altona*, 29.
Cooee ex *Neuminster*, 32-33.
Coolcha, 8, 41.
Corinda, 47.
Culburra, 7, 41.

69

D

Dalton Hall became *Australstream*, 9, 24, 25.
Delungra, 7, 12, 43.
Demosthenes, 16.
Dilga, 7, 43.
Dimitrios N. Rallas ex *Liberta*, ex *Australfield*, ex *Vermont*, 17.
Dinoga became *Colac, Easby, Clydebreeze*, 7, 12-13, 43.
Dongarra ex *Stolzenfels*, 33.
Dromana, 7, 42-43.
Duke of Westminster, 3.
Dumosa, 7, 42-43.
Dundula, 7, 43.

E

Easby ex *Colac* became *Clyde Breeze*, 43.
Echuca became *Mareeba*, 8, 12, 18, 44-45.
Echunga, 8, 44, 47.
Elouera became *Iron Prince*, 8, 12, 44-45.
Emden, 14.
Emita became *Milora*, 12-13, 44-45.
Enoggera became *Mildura*, 12, 44-45.
Enterprise, 15.
Erina became *Eugowra*, 44.
Eromanga became *Maranoa*, 13, 44, 47.
Erriba became *Murada*, 12, 44.
Esperance Bay I became *Arawa*, 16-17, 50.
Esperance Bay II ex *Hobson's Bay*, 16-17.
Eudunda became *Mangola*, 8, 13, 44-45.
Eugowra ex *Erina*, 44, 47.
Eurelia became *Mungana*, 8, 12, 44-45, 47.
Eurimbla became *Iron Master*, 8, 12, 44-45.
Euripedes became *Akaroa*, 16.
Euroa became *Iron Crown*, 12, 44, 46.
Euwarra became *Iron Knob*, 8, 11-12, 44, 46.

F

Ferndale, 9-10, 14-15, 53-54, 58.
Finland, 4.
Fordsdale, 9-10, 14, 52-54.
Friedrichsruh ex *Frust Bismarck*, 11.
Furst Bismarck became *Friedrichsruh*, 11.

G

Garlock, 9.
General Degoute ex *Australstream*, 9, 24, 25.
Germania, 31 became *Mawatta*, 31.
Gilgai, 31.
Gladstone became *Akuna II*, 27.
Griefswald became *Corina*, 28.

H

Hessen, 4, 29.
Hobart became *Baranbah*, 33.
Hobson's Bay became *Esperance Bay II*, 16.
Horai Maru ex *Indarra*, 52

I

Indarra became *Horai Maru*, 52.
Iron Chief ex *Mandy Lodge*, 58.
Iron Crown ex *Euroa*, 12, 46.
Iron Knob ex *Euwarra*, 12, 46.
Iron Master ex *Eurimbla*, 12, 45.
Iron Prince ex *Elouera*, became *Kembla Breeze*, 12, 45.
Iron Warrior, 13, 47-48.
Ishikari Maru ex *Australrange*, 21.

J

Jervis Bay, 15, 17, 48, 50.
John Murray ex *Loch Ryan*, 39-40.
Jurumba, 2.

K

Kanowna, 51.
Karuah, 2.
Kembla Breeze ex *Iron Prince*, 12, 45.
Kirkoswald became *Australmead*, 24.
Komet became *Una*, 27.
Koolinda, 31.
Koombana, 31.
Kormoran, 18, 46.
Kotka ex *Albertina*, 28.
Kyarra, 51, 52.
Kyogle, 2.

L

Lady Loch, 2.
Largs Bay, 10, 17, 48.
Liberta, ex *Australfield* became *Dimitrios N. Rallas*, 17, 25.
Lienta, 2.
Loch Ryan became *John Murray*, 39.
Loongana, 58.
Lothringen became *Moora*, 33.
Louis Thierault, 40.

M

Mandy Lodge became *Iron Chief*, 58.
Mangola ex *Eudunda*, 13, 45.
Maranoa ex *Eromanga*, 3, 12, 47.
Mareeba ex *Echuca*, 12, 18, 46.
Matina, 37-39.

Mawatta ex *Germania*, 31.
Melbourne, H.M.A.S., 30.
Melbourne became *Boonah*, 29-30.
Merimbula, 2, 59.
Miho Maru ex *Australpool*, 18.
Mildura ex *Enoggera*, 12, 45.
Milora ex *Emita*, 13, 45.
Misaka Maru ex *Australcrag*, 20.
Moana, 40.
Moira, 31.
Moora ex *Lothringen*, 33.
Moreton Bay, 10, 14, 17, 48, 57.
Mungana ex *Eurelia*, 45, 47.
Murada ex *Erriba*, 46.

N

Nereus ex *Boorara*, 32.
Nestor, 13.
Neuminster became *Cooee*, 32.
Niagara, 11.

O

Oberhausen became *Booral*, 33.
Olinda became *Cardinia*, 8, 40.
Orient, 3.
Orion, 16.
Osnabruck became *Calcutta*, 33.

P

Parattah ex *Berlin*, 6, 27, 32.
Paringa, 58.
Paroo, 51.
Pfalz became *Boorara*, 4, 10, 42.
Pilbarra, 51.
Prinz Zigmund became *Bambra*, 10, 31.

R

Rawalpindi, 17.
Rosario ex *Witell* became *Albertina*, 28.

S

Scharzfels became *Araluen*, 13.
Shandon ex *Victor*, 6, 40.
Sir William Matthews, 6.
Slavol, 15.
Speedway, 40.
Strathairly became *Australpool*, 18, 21.
Strathavon became *Australford*, 23.
Strathbeg became *Australmount*, 22.
Strathdee became *Australrange*, 20.
Strathendrick became *Australdale*, 19.
Strathesk became *Australbrook*, 19.

Strathleven became *Australcrag*, 19-20.
Strathord became *Australglen*, 24.
Strathspey became *Australpeak*, 22.
Stolzenfels became *Dongarra*, 33.
Sumatra became *Barungra*, 33.
Sydney, H.M.A.S., 14, 58.

T

Thames, 9.
Themistocles, 17.
Toromeo ex *Tiberius*, 33.
Torres Breeze, 45.
Tiberius became *Toromeo*, 33.
Tural became *Carawa*, 28-29.

U

Uga Maru ex *Australbrook*, 19.
Ulysses, 13.
Una ex *Komet* became *Akuna I*, 27.

V

Vermont became *Australfield*, 9, 17, 25.
Victor became *Shandon*, 40.
Victoria, 27.

W

Wildenfels became *Gilgah*, 31.
Witell ex *Bakara* became *Rosario*, 28.

INDEX TO ILLUSTRATIONS

Akuna, Port Phillip pilot ship	7	*Loch Ryan*	1
Arawa, ex *Esperance Bay I*	21	*Loongana*	25
Ardongorm	12		
Australbrook ex *Strathesk*	10	*Mareeba,* A.U.S.N. Co,	16
Australcrag ex *Strathleven*	8	Maryborough, Queensland	13,14,15
Australpeak ex *Strathspey*	9	*Matina,* 1910	29
Australpool ex *Strathairly*	11	*Melbourne*	4
Australport ex *Ardongorm*	12	*Milora,* scuttling of	17
Australia I	33		
Australia, HMAS, scuttling of	26	*Nestor*	38
Barambah, ex s.s. *Hobart*	5	*Oberhausen*	6
Boonah, ex s.s. *Melbourne*	4		
Booral, ex s.s. *Oberhausen*	6	*Pericles*	37
Ceramic	36	*Quetta*	35
Echuca, being launched	13	*Shandon*	2
Echuca, raising steam for trials	14	*Sophocles*	28
Echuca, proceeding down Mary River	15	*Strathairly*	11
Echuca, s.s. *Mareeba*	16	*Strathesk*	10
Esperance Bay I	21	*Strathleven*	8
		Strathspey	9
Ferndale	18	*Sydney,* HMAS	27
Fordsdale	19		
		Tarawa ex *Tural*	3
Hobart	5	*Taroona*	31
		Themistocles	22, 34
Indarra, A.U.S.N. Co, 1921	23	*Tural*	3
Indarra as *Horai Maru*	24		
		Ulysses	38
Jervis Bay	20	*Una*	7
Kanowna	30	*Victoria*	39
Komet	7		
		Waratah	32

Note. The Characters are to be inscribed only in the appropriate ornamented spaces below. All of these spaces which are not filled in with particulars of Character must be marked over with a thick Cross in Ink by the Superintendent, Consul, or other Shipping Officer, before the Certificate is given out of his possession.

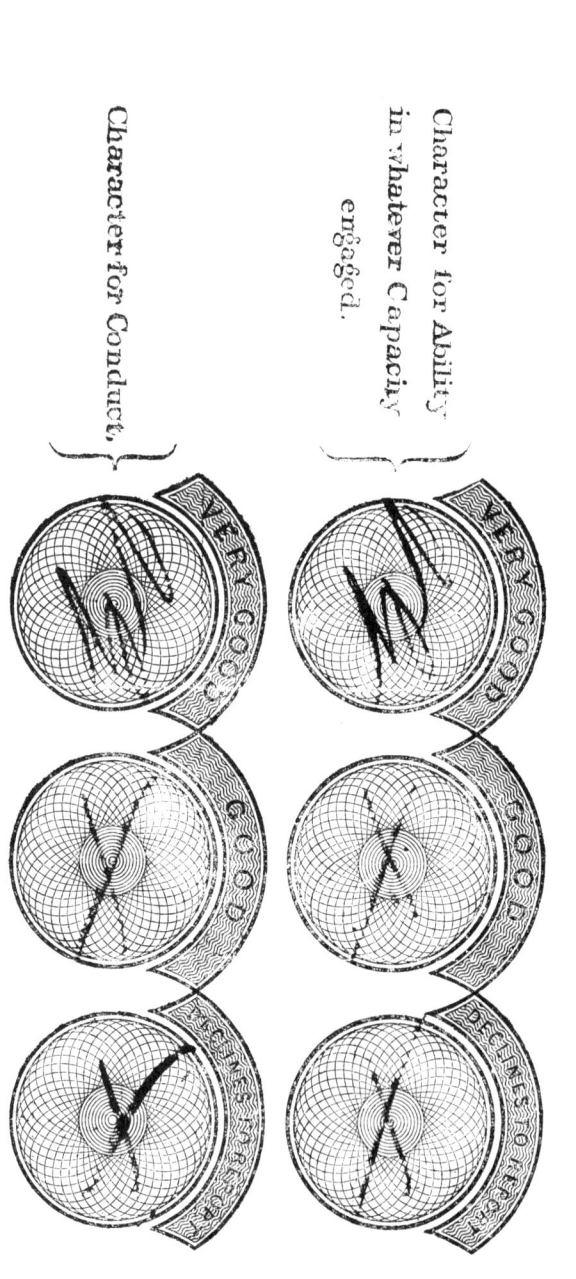

Character for Ability in whatever Capacity engaged.

Character for Conduct.

[VERY GOOD] [VERY GOOD]
[GOOD] [GOOD]
[DECLINES TO REPORT] [DECLINES TO REPORT]

✳✳ CARE IS TO BE TAKEN THAT THE ABOVE CIRCLES ARE CROSSED THROUGH OR FILLED IN